# CHECK YOUR TAX

## THE
## COMPLETE GUIDE

# 2008–2009

# CHECK YOUR TAX

# THE
# COMPLETE GUIDE

# 2008–2009

*by*
GRAHAM M KITCHEN, FCA

foulsham

LONDON • NEW YORK • TORONTO • SYDNEY

# foulsham

The Publishing House, Bennetts Close,
Cippenham, Slough, Berkshire SL1 5AP, England

ISBN: 978-0-572-03399-6

Printed in Great Britain by Creative Print & Design (Wales), Ebbw Vale.

# Contents

# CHAPTER 1

# Budget summary

Although the changes proposed in the March 2008 budget and pre-budget report of October 2007 are dealt with throughout this book, this chapter summarises the main points and other relevant legislation that has occurred since the last edition of this book, and gives references to the pages that deal specifically with each topic.

As seems to have become the pattern in recent budget speeches, many of the announcements do not apply to the 2008–2009 tax year but to future years.

## Personal allowances

The allowances for 2008–2009 are as follows:

| | £ | Page No. |
|---|---|---|
| Personal allowances | | |
| age under 65 | 5,435 | 92 |
| age 65–74* | 9,030 | 111 |
| age 75 or over* | 9,180 | 111 |
| Married couple's allowance for those born before 6 April 1935: | | |
| age 65–74* | 6,535† | 111 |
| age 75 or over* | 6,625† | 111 |
| minimum amount | 2,540 | 111 |
| *Income limit | 21,800 | 111 |
| Maintenance relief – maximum relief if born before 6 April 1935 | 2,540† | 88 |
| Blind person's allowance | 1,800 | 93 |

†Relief at only 10 per cent.

## Future personal allowances

In addition to announcing the personal allowances for 2008–2009 (see above), the personal allowances for people aged 65 to 74 will be increased to reach £9,770 in 2011–2012; and for those aged 75 or over it is anticipated that their personal allowance will rise to £10,000 by 2011–2012.

## Rates of tax

The starting rate of 10 per cent is abolished for earned income (including pensions) as from 6 April 2008, with the basic rate being reduced to 20 per cent from 22 per cent on the first £36,000 of income. The higher rate remains at 40 per cent.

There will be a new 10 per cent starting rate for savings income only, with a limit of £2,320. If an individual's taxable non-savings income is above this limit then the 10 per cent savings rate will not be applicable. There are no changes to the 10 per cent dividend ordinary rate or the 32.5 per cent dividend upper rate.

## Tax return deadlines

The latest dates for the 2007–2008 tax return to be submitted are to be 31 October 2008 for paper returns and 31 January 2009 for electronic submissions, after which penalties and interest may be applied.

## Child tax credit and working tax credit

There are increases in most of the credits for 2008–2009. From April 2009, the child tax credit for low and middle income families will rise by £50 a year above inflation.

## Child benefit and guardian's allowance

There are inflation increases for 2008–2009 but from April 2009 child benefit for the first child will be increased by £20 a week.

## Child trust funds

It was confirmed again in the budget that further sums will be paid in 2009 when a child reaches the age of seven.

## State pension rates

These are to increase from 1 April 2008 to £90.70 per week for a single person and £145 per week for couples.

## Pension credit

There are increases in the guaranteed element from 6 April 2008.

## Winter fuel payments

Winter fuel payment for the over 60-year-olds increases to £250 for 2008–2009 and to £400 for those over 80 years old. There can still only be one beneficiary per household.

109

## Gift aid

Although the basic rate of tax has been reduced to 20 per cent for 2008–2009, repayment of gift aid to charities will be made at a transitional rate of 22 per cent for three years from 2008–2009

89

## Company car benefits

Most of the taxable benefits on company cars remains unaltered for 2008–2009 but a new lower rate of 10 per cent (13 per cent for diesels) will apply from 6 April 2008 on vehicles with $CO_2$ emissions of 120 g/km or less. The current lower threshold of 140 g/km will reduce to 130 from 6 April 2010.

66

## Company private fuel benefits

The fuel scale charge base figure will increase from £14,400 to £16,900 a year from 6 April 2008.

68

## National insurance contributions

From 6 April 2008, there are changes to the lower and upper earnings limits for employees' contributions. The main percentage rates remain unaltered. With the £100 increase in the upper earnings limit, this means that this extra £100 earned will have national insurance levied at 11 per cent rather than 1 per cent. The upper earnings limit for employees and the self-employed is increased from £34,840 to £40,040.

133

## Individual savings accounts (ISAs)

From 2008–2009, the distinction between maxi and mini ISAs has been abolished and the maximum annual investment limit increased to £7,200 with the maximum cash component being £3,600. This is the first increase in the investment levels for eight years.

160

## Capital gains tax

Tapering relief and indexation is being abolished from 6 April 2008.

The annual exemption limit for 2008–2009 is increased to £9,600 for individuals and £4,800 for trusts.

The tax rate for capital gains for 2008–2009 is to be a flat 18 per cent with a new entrepreneurs' relief giving an effective rate of 10 per cent up to a maximum gain of £1 million.

## Enterprise investment schemes

There are increases in the investment limits for 2008–2009.

## Enterprise management incentive share options

From 6 April 2008, the individual grant limit for shares increases to £120,000.

## Pension scheme allowances

For 2008–2009, the annual allowance is increased to £235,000 and the lifetime allowance to £1,650,000.

## Inheritance tax

The exempt threshold for 2008–2009 is confirmed at £312,000 for individuals. This is to increase to £325,000 for 2009–2010 and £350,000 for 2010–2011.

The announcement made on October 2007 that any unused exemption allowance on the death of one partner to a marriage or civil partnership can be utilised by the remaining partner was confirmed in the budget.

## Capital allowances

The writing down allowance for plant and machinery will reduce from 25 per cent to 20 per cent from April 2008. There are increases for long-life assets and certain other assets. First-year allowances for small and medium companies are being replaced by a new annual investment allowance on plant and machinery regardless of the size of the company.

Plant and machinery capital allowance pools of £1,000 or less can be written off.

From April 2009, there will be changes in the capital allowance rates for cars favouring low-emission vehicles.

## Research and development tax credits

From April 2008, these will rise from 125 per cent to 130 per cent for large companies and from 150 per cent to 175 per cent for small to medium companies.

## Corporation tax

The main corporation tax rate for 2008–2009 will be reduced from 30 per cent to 28 per cent with the small companies rate increasing from 20 per cent to 21 per cent and further increasing to 22 per cent from April 2009.

## VAT

There are increases in the turnover thresholds for registration and de-registration effective from 1 April 2008.

## Stamp duty

There are no changes in stamp duty levels.

## Non-domiciled residents

Non-domiciled residents, after living in the UK for seven out of the last ten years, will have to pay an annual tax charge of £30,000 to retain their existing tax privileges, or be faced with paying such UK tax on their *worldwide* income. This change commences from 6 April 2008.

## Tax inspections

There were proposals in the budget to broaden the powers of tax inspectors to enable them to make unannounced visits to taxpayer's homes or offices when they suspect evasion of tax.

## Landfill tax

This tax will increase from £24 per tonne to £32 as from 1 April 2008 and to £40 from 1 April 2009.

# CHAPTER 2

# How much for you and how much for the tax inspector

Almost everyone receives income that is liable to income tax in one form or another. You may find, however, that you can avoid paying tax, or at least reduce your tax bill, by claiming certain allowances, by offsetting various types of expense or by changing where you invest your savings.

The allowances and expenses you can claim are dealt with later in this book. This chapter tells you what income is free from tax and what income is taxable.

Taxable income can be divided into two types: earned income and unearned, or investment, income.

## The tax inspector can claim part of the following types of income

### Earned income

Annuities from past jobs.

Benefits – private use of firm's car, fuel, services generally.

Benefits of cheap or interest-free loans from your employer for a non-qualifying purpose (see page 70).

Bereavement allowance.

Carer's allowance.

Commission, including that from mail order companies, etc.

Compensation for loss of office (but see page 73).

Earnings from casual work and tips.

Expense allowances if not spent entirely on firm's business.

Holiday pay.

Incapacity benefit – except for the first 28 weeks.

Incentive schemes.

Income from furnished and unfurnished accommodation (but see page 84).

Income from overseas employment and pensions.

Income withdrawals from a delayed annuity pension plan.

Industrial death benefit if paid as a pension.

Jobseeker's allowance – up to the taxable maximum.

Luncheon vouchers – excess over 15p a day per person.

Maternity, paternity or adoption pay (statutory).
Pensions – from the State, previous employers or your own
    scheme.
Profits from trades or professions.
Redundancy (see page 73).
Royalties earned from your own work.
Salaries, fees and bonuses.
Sick pay (statutory).
Stipends received by the clergy.
Wages.
Widow's pension.
Widowed mother's and widowed parent's allowance.

## Investment income

Annuities purchased.
Bank interest.
Building society cash windfalls on a merger.
Building society interest.
Dividends.
Gains from certain non-qualifying insurance policies.
Interest on National Savings income bonds and capital bonds.
Income from overseas investment and property.
Income from trusts and from estates of deceased persons.
National Savings interest on all savings accounts, but not the first
    £70 per person per year on ordinary accounts.
Rents and 'key' money (except holiday lettings) after expenses.
Reverse premiums.
Royalties – bought or inherited.
Stock or scrip dividends – dividends paid in shares instead of cash.

## The various rates of tax are shown on page 187.

## The following income is all yours – it is free of income tax

Adoption allowances under approved schemes.
Annuities resulting from gallantry awards.
Armed forces operational allowance (from 1 April 2006).
Attendance allowance.
Awards for damages.
Bereavement payment (lump sum).
Betting and pools winnings.
Car parking benefits.
Child benefit and allowances.

Child dependency additions paid with many State benefits.

Child tax credit.

Child trust fund proceeds, after the age of 18.

Christmas bonus for pensioners from the State.

Compensation for loss of office and redundancy pay up to £30,000 (but see page 73).

Compensation for mis-sold personal pensions and personal injury.

Council tax benefit.

Disability living allowance.

Disability or wounds pensions.

Education grants and awards from a local authority or school.

Endowment policies.

Ex-gratia payments from your employer up to £30,000 (but see page 73).

Family income supplement and family credit.

Gifts for employees provided by third parties if under £250 a year.

Gratuities from the armed forces.

Guardian's allowance.

Home improvement, repair and insulation grants.

Housing benefit.

Incapacity benefit (if previously received as invalidity benefit at 12 April 1995 for the same incapacity and first 28 weeks of new claims).

Income support.

Individual savings accounts income (ISAs).

Industrial injury benefits.

Insurance policy benefits for accident, sickness, disability or unemployment.

Insurance bond withdrawals up to 5 per cent a year, but a portion may be subject to tax on redemption.

Interest on delayed tax repayments.

Interest from National Savings certificates.

Invalidity pension.

Jobseeker's allowance over the taxable maximum.

Life assurance policy bonuses and profits.

Long-service awards up to £50 for each year of service (but not cash).

Lotto winnings.

Lump sums from an approved pension scheme on retirement.

Luncheon vouchers up to 15p per person per day (any cash allowance would be taxable).

Maintenance or alimony.

Maternity allowance (statutory).

Miners' coal allowance, whether in cash or kind.

National Savings interest up to £70 per person per year on ordinary accounts only.

National Savings certificates' increase in value.

Paternity allowance (statutory).

Pension credit.

Pensions from Austria or Germany to victims of Nazi persecution.

Personal equity plan dividends reinvested.

Premium bond prizes.

Provident benefits up to £4,000 for lump sum payments.

Purchased life annuities – the capital proportion of yearly amount.

Redundancy pay (statutory) (but see page 73).

Rent and council tax rebates.

Rent-a-room relief up to £4,250 a year (see page 85).

SAYE schemes – interest and bonus.

Severe disablement allowances.

Shares issued under an approved share incentive scheme, authorised by a tax office, up to a value of £3,000 or, if greater, 10 per cent of the employee's earnings, subject to a maximum of £8,000. After five years the proceeds are tax free.

Share option profits made under the SAYE scheme previously run by National Savings and Investments – no income tax but capital gains tax may be payable.

Sickness benefits under an insurance policy for up to 12 months where the premiums are paid by the employee.

Social fund payments.

Strike and unemployment pay from a trade union.

Student grants.

Subsidised or free bus travel to work.

Termination payments up to £30,000 (but see page 73).

TESSA interest if kept for the full period.

TOISA interest.

Training allowances.

Vaccine damage (lump sum).

Venture capital trust dividends (but see page 163).

War disablement pensions.

War widow's pension.

Winter fuel and cold weather payment for pensioners.

Working tax credit.

# CHAPTER 3

# Tax forms and what to do with them

## Tax returns

You must fill in a tax return if the tax office send you one, or you are a higher rate taxpayer, or if you are in partnership or self-employed, or you have income to declare on which tax is due. You will also want to fill in a tax return if you have paid too much tax and are due a refund.

If you need a tax return and haven't received one, then contact the tax office that deals with your employer's PAYE or, if you are self-employed or unemployed, then contact your local tax office. There are time limits after which you will be charged penalties and interest (see page 35).

Chapter 4 takes you step by step through all aspects of the tax return and any supplementary pages. If you need supplementary tax return pages, telephone the order line on 0845 9000 404 or download them from **www.hmrc.gov.uk**.

There is also a free tax office helpline on 0845 9000 444.

## Short tax return (SA210)

Some taxpayers receive a new 'short tax return'. As its name implies, it is much simpler and shorter than the full self-assessment tax return and it is sent to those taxpayers whose tax affairs are fairly straightforward.

You must **not** use the short tax return if you:

- were a company director at any time in the tax year;
- received a lump sum from an employer unless it was a redundancy payment below £30,000;
- were self-employed and had more than one business; or your turnover was more than £15,000, or you changed your accounting date or want to offset losses;
- want to offset losses or pension contributions;
- were in partnership;

- are repaying a student loan;
- were involved in share options or received gains from life policies;
- received property income of more than £15,000, or had more than one property, or had furnished holiday letting income;
- received income from abroad or from a trust, etc.;
- were not resident or domiciled in the UK.

Do remember that you cannot file a short tax return electronically. If you do wish to file under this method you must request a full self assessment tax return.

There is a free tax office helpline for the short tax return on 0845 302 1486.

## PAYE coding notice (form P2)

Don't just put this in a drawer and forget about it. Check it as explained on page 99.

Ensure that your employer has been notified of any alteration in your tax code by the tax office. You should write to your tax office if you disagree with any figure.

## Annual earnings (form P60)

Your employer has by law to give you this form by 31 May after the end of every tax year. It shows your earnings from that employment, the total PAYE deducted in the year and total contributions made by you and your employer for national insurance.

Check the form to see if you can claim some tax back as shown in Chapter 11 (see page 101).

## Income tax repayment claim (form R40)

This will be sent to you by your tax office if most of your income has had tax deducted before receipt and you normally have to claim tax back at the end of each tax year.

There is a free taxback helpline on 0845 0776 543.

## Enquiry form (form 33)

This form is issued by the tax office covering your home address or a tax office that knows that you have been paid income by someone in their area. Complete and return it as soon as possible otherwise there could be delays in settling your tax matters in the future.

## Notice of income paid gross (form RU6(M))

This is sometimes sent to people who have registered with banks or building societies to have their income paid gross – that is without having tax deducted.

Fill in the form carefully because the tax office send it to you to check your total income to make sure that you are not liable to pay tax (see page 114).

## Notice of employee leaving (form P45)

This form is issued to you by your employer when you leave. If you are immediately going to another job, hand parts 2 and 3 to your new employer. Otherwise, send them to the tax office shown on the form, together with a letter stating that you are at present unemployed, to see if you can claim a repayment of tax. Keep part 1A as you will need to refer to this when you fill in your tax return.

If you do not have this form, or if you lose it, then you will have to complete a questionnaire (form P46) obtainable from your new employer. Your employer will send this to your tax office and use a temporary PAYE code until you either provide a P45 form or the tax office advises him of a new code for you.

## Return of expenses and allowances (form P11D)

This is an annual form to be completed by an employer for each employee who has received earnings, expenses and potential benefits of £8,500 or more a year. It must also be completed for all directors regardless of their earnings level. The form will detail all benefits and expenses that you were paid or given by your employer in the tax year (see Chapter 5, page 65).

There is also a form P9D for employees earning at a rate of less than £8,500 a year who have received benefits, etc. that are taxable.

## Retirement enquiry form (form P161)

This form is sent to everyone who is reaching statutory retirement age and should be completed and returned to ensure that you get the correct tax allowances (see page 108).

## Subcontractors in the construction industry

If you are providing services to a company involved in construction work you will normally have tax deducted from your earnings at the rate of 18 per cent before the money is paid to you. You will have received CIS25 vouchers showing the tax deducted. Send the vouchers in with your tax return. The tax return makes provision for you to declare this income, and the tax deducted, so that you are not taxed on the same amount twice. If you have established a record of regular work (and have conformed with the tax rules) for three consecutive years, then you can apply to the tax office for a CIS6 certificate that will enable you to be paid gross – there are also minimum turnover levels depending on whether you are an individual or a company.

There is a helpline telephone number: 0845 733 5588.

## Self assessment – tax calculation (form SA 302)

This notice summarises your income tax situation and shows how much is due or has been overpaid. You must check it carefully and ensure that the figures correspond to those stated in your tax return.

As well as setting out how your tax liability (or refund) is calculated, there will quite often be comments explaining certain figures or responding to queries you have raised. It is easy to overlook these comments as the form is prepared on a computer and they don't stand out as they would in a conventional letter, therefore check the form carefully.

The calculation will not reflect any payments on account you may have made and you will therefore need to check the figures with your statement of account (see below) to confirm your tax position.

If you cannot understand the calculations, or you have a query, telephone the helpline on 0845 9000 444.

If you cannot submit your tax return because you have information outstanding, you should still estimate your tax liability and make payments by the due date to avoid interest and surcharges arising on any amount unpaid. You would also avoid the £100 late filing penalty by doing this as the penalty is restricted to the actual tax outstanding.

## Self assessment – statement of account (form SA 300)

This statement, sent out by your tax office, shows how much tax is due and when it should be paid; it will also show, where applicable, any payments that are due on account.

If the statement shows you have paid too much tax and the overpayment has not been refunded to you, contact your tax office to request a repayment.

If you have registered to file electronically, you can access your statement at any time on the website at **www.hmrc.gov.uk**.

One of the advantages of the self assessment tax system is that an individual now only deals with one tax office – in the past, particularly in the case of pensioners or those who have more than one employer, you could have been dealing with two or three tax offices.

## General comments

You should not ignore any form or communication from the tax authorities but should deal with it immediately, either by replying yourself or passing it on to the tax adviser who deals with your tax affairs.

The deadlines for returning your 2008 self assessment tax return are 31 October 2008 (or two months after the date the return form was sent to you, if later than this) or 31 January 2009 if you plan to file electronically.

Interest and penalties for late submission of your tax return or tax payments are now very stringent (see page 35).

# How to fill in your 2008 tax return

Not everyone automatically receives a tax return to fill in every year, but if you do receive one, you must complete it and return it to your tax office. The tax office relies on the fact that it is the taxpayer's responsibility to advise them of any changes in sources of income or claims for expenses and allowances. You may, of course, ask for a tax return to complete if you do not receive one, by telephoning your local tax office or the tax office that deals with your PAYE if you are employed.

A husband and wife, and civil partners, are treated as individuals in their own right for tax purposes, getting their own tax return, being responsible for their own tax affairs and getting their own individual tax allowances and exemptions.

The tax year runs from 6 April in one year to 5 April in the following year.

The tax return has been completely redesigned for 2008 and if your tax affairs are not particularly complicated then there may be fewer questions to answer than in the past.

The main tax return (SA100) only covers your income from savings and investments, pension income, any State benefits received and any miscellaneous income. It also covers your claim for any allowances or reliefs.

There is a new set of separate pages included with your tax return which has not appeared in previous years. It is called *SA101 Additional information*. You may need to complete these if:

- You have income that is not covered in the main return (such as income from Government securities, share schemes).
- You want to claim other tax reliefs (for example, married couple's allowance, maintenance payments).
- You want to claim tax losses.
- You have overseas pensions.

Don't worry about these pages. Progress through the tax return as indicated on the following pages and you will be told if you need to use these additional information pages.

All other types of income and claims for expenses are covered in one of the eight sets of supplementary pages detailed on page TR2 of your tax return.

**Read through the questions on page TR2 and tick the 'yes', 'no' and 'number' boxes as appropriate.**

For clarification, these supplementary pages are summarised here with the page number in this book that deals with them in more detail. If you had more than one employer, self-employment or partnership then you need a separate set of the appropriate pages for each business.

Page
No.

### Employment (SA102)

You will need these sheets if you were an employee or a director or an agency worker in the tax year, or if you received expenses payments or benefits from a former employer.                36

### Self-employment (SA103)

These pages cover a situation where you work for yourself. There are two types – the short form reproduced in this book is for businesses that are fairly straightforward with a turnover of less than £64,000 a year, and the full version is for all other businesses.                39

### Partnership (SA104)

If you were in a partnership, these are the pages you will need. As above, there are short and full versions.                42

### UK property (SA105)

These pages are needed if you had income from any UK property or land.                44

### Foreign (SA106)

These pages in general cover foreign income and gains from overseas – do not include income from employment or self-employment from overseas – that income should be declared in one of the supplementary pages referred to above.                47

## Trusts etc. (SA107)

These pages cover income received from a trust, settlement or a deceased person's estate.

## Capital gains summary (SA108)

If you made capital gains, or you wish to claim an allowable capital loss, then use these pages to give the details. However, capital gains is a complicated tax and you should refer to Chapter 15 in this book to see whether you need to fill in these sheets, for not all capital gains have to be declared.

## Non-resident (SA109)

You will need these pages if you were not resident, ordinary resident or domiciled in the UK or you had dual residency.

If you have answered 'yes' to any of these questions and you do not have the appropriate supplementary pages attached to your tax return, then telephone 0845 9000 404 or fax 0845 9000 604 and request the required sheets.

Blind persons requiring Braille versions should contact their local office.

## The main tax return

**Having completed all this preparatory checking, you can now start filling in your main tax return.**

Start by completing your personal details on page TR1 and then complete the student loan repayments section on page TR2 if it is applicable to you (see page 153 of this book for more details).

### Student loan repayments

| 1 | If your employer has deducted Student Loan repayments enter the amount deducted | 2 | If you have received notification from the Student Loans Company that repayment of an Income Contingent Student Loan began before 6 April 2008, put 'X' in the box |
|---|---|---|---|
| | £ . 0 0 | | |

Now fill in the **Income** section of the return – starting on page TR3.

### UK interest, etc. and dividends

| 1 | UK bank, building society, unit trust, etc. interest/amount which has been taxed already - *the net amount after tax* | 4 | Dividends from authorised unit trusts and open-ended investment companies |
|---|---|---|---|
| | £ . 0 0 | | £ . 0 0 |
| 2 | Untaxed UK interest etc. (amounts that have not been taxed at all) - *the total amount* | 5 | Foreign dividends (up to £300) - *the amount in sterling before foreign tax was taken off. Do not include this amount in the Foreign pages* |
| | £ . 0 0 | | £ . 0 0 |
| 3 | Dividends from UK companies - *do not include the tax credit. Property Income Dividends (PIDs) go in box 15 below* | 6 | Tax taken off foreign dividends (the sterling equivalent) |
| | £ . 0 0 | | £ . 0 0 |

You may need the following paperwork in order to summarise the figures required:

| | |
|---|---|
| Interest statements and tax deduction certificates from UK banks, building societies and deposit takers | |
| Details of any National Savings investments | |
| Dividend vouchers | |

More details regarding the information to be declared under this section can be found on pages 82–83 of this book together with some tax saving tips. If you have investments in joint names refer to page 82.

Note that the term 'UK bank' includes National Savings and Investments.

You do not have to declare any interest in this section that is exempt from tax (for example, interest from ISAs, PEPs, SAYE schemes, National Savings certificate interest, the first £70 of interest on National Savings ordinary accounts).

Although the tax office does not want you to list all of your individual dividends and interest in this tax form – you only have to put in the totals – you will need to keep the details in case the tax office ask for them. Use the working sheet on page 173 to keep a record.

**Box 1.** Show the actual amount of interest you received after tax had been deducted. Include the interest element of purchased life annuities here, but exclude the capital element (see page 115).

**Box 2.** Show the total interest you received that did *not* have any tax deducted.

**Box 3.** This is for dividends from UK companies.

**Box 4.** This is for dividends from authorised unit trusts and open-ended investment companies – show the amounts actually received.

If you have any dividends from overseas you can enter the gross amount in box 4 if the total is less than £300; (if it is more then you will have to complete the *Foreign* supplementary pages (see page 47).

**Box 6.** Any tax deducted should be shown in box 6.

Do not include interest from Government stocks (gilt-edged securities) in this section – this needs to be declared in the *Additional information* supplementary pages (see page 59).

## UK pensions, annuities and other State benefits received

| | |
|---|---|
| **7** State Pension - *the amount due for the year (not the weekly amount)* £ · 0 0 | **11** Tax taken off box 10 £ · 0 0 |
| **8** State Pension lump sum £ · 0 0 | **12** Taxable Incapacity Benefit - *the total amount before tax was taken off* £ · 0 0 |
| **9** Tax taken off box 8 £ · 0 0 | **13** Tax taken off box 12 £ · 0 0 |
| **10** Pensions (other than State Pension), retirement annuities and taxable triviality payments - *give details of the payers, amounts paid and tax deducted in box 19 on page TR 6* £ · 0 0 | **14** Total of any other taxable State Pensions and benefits £ · 0 0 |

You may need the following paperwork to summarise the figures required:

| | |
|---|---|
| Your State pension book or statements | |
| A P60 form or certificate of tax deducted in the case of any other pension | |
| Benefit office or DWP statements in respect of any incapacity benefit or other taxable State benefit or jobseeker's allowance | |

More information and tax tips on the figures to go in this section can be found in Chapter 7 on page 82.

**Box 7.** This is not just for the basic State pension – you need to include any additional or graduated State pension. Do not include the State Christmas bonus or winter fuel payment as they are not taxable. A married woman should enter in her own tax return any pension she receives even if it is paid as a result of her husband's contributions.

**Box 8.** If you have deferred taking the State pension and have now received a lump sum payment, this goes in here.

**Box 9.** Note any tax deducted.

**Box 10.** All other pensions you receive should be added together (before any tax deducted) and entered here.

**Box 11.** Enter the tax deducted.

**Box 19.** The tax office suggest you give all the details in box 19, although there is not much room. Some UK pensions for service to an overseas government have a 10 per cent exemption from UK tax, in which case only 90 per cent of the pension needs to be declared – clearly state this on the form.

Use the working sheet on page 178 of this book to collate the various pension amounts. Remember that pensions received *from abroad* should be entered in the *Foreign* supplementary pages of your tax return, not in this section.

**Box 12.** Only incapacity benefit received after the first 28 weeks (or commenced before 13 April 2005) is taxable and needs to be entered.

**Box 13.** Enter the amount of the tax deducted.

**Box 14.** Any other State pensions or benefits received that are not covered in the earlier boxes should be entered here. See page 76.

## Other UK income not included on supplementary pages

Do not use this section for income that should be returned on supplementary pages. Share schemes, gilts, stock dividends, life insurance gains and certain other kinds of income go on the *Additional information* pages in the Tax Return pack.

15 Other taxable income - *before expenses and tax taken off*

£ · 0 0

16 Total amount of allowable expenses - *read page TRG 11 of the guide*

£ · 0 0

17 Any tax taken off box 15

£ · 0 0

18 Benefit from pre-owned assets - *read page TRG 11 of the guide*

£ · 0 0

19 Description of boxes 15 and 18 income - *if there is not enough space here please give details in the 'Any other information' box on page TR 6*

This section basically covers any other type of income that has not been declared above, or is not covered by the supplementary pages, which you would have ticked on the check list on page TR2 of the tax return.

**Box 15.** This is particularly useful for declaring any miscellaneous income from casual work, insurance or mail order commission, royalties, freelance income etc. Use the working sheets at the back of this book on page 174 to add together the various types of income – it is only the total that needs to be entered in the return. Rather surprisingly Box 15 also covers here any dividends or distributions from real estate investment trusts (REITs).

**Box 16.** This gives you the opportunity of claiming any expenses against any of the income declared in box 15. See Chapter 6 for guidance as to what you can claim and any tax tips. Collate your expenses in the working sheets on page 176, as the tax office may ask for more specific details at a later date, and put the total in this box.

**Box 17.** If any tax had been deducted before you received any income, show the total tax here.

**Box 18.** Benefits from pre-owned assets arises from the inheritance legislation and is now incorporated in this section of the tax return and any such benefits need to be declared in box 18. This subject is dealt with on page 145. Your calculation as to how you arrive at this figure needs to be shown in box 19, not in this section but on page TR6 of your tax return.

**Box 19.** This enables you state the broad details of the income declared in boxes 15 and 18 – you just need to state from where the income arose, e.g. 'royalties £251'.

**The tax return now covers reliefs and allowances that you can claim as a deduction from your income.**

### Pension contributions

Paying into registered pension schemes and overseas pension schemes

Do not include payments you make to your employer's pension scheme which are deducted from your pay before tax or payments made by your employer. Boxes to return pension savings tax charges and taxable lump sums from overseas pensions schemes are on the *Additional information* pages.

| | |
|---|---|
| **1** Payments to registered pension schemes where basic rate tax relief will be claimed by your pension provider (called 'relief at source'). Enter the payments and basic rate tax<br><br>£ ⬚⬚⬚⬚⬚⬚⬚ · 0 0 | **3** Payments to your employer's scheme which were not deducted from your pay before tax<br><br>£ ⬚⬚⬚⬚⬚⬚⬚ · 0 0 |
| **2** Payments to a retirement annuity contract where basic rate tax relief will not be claimed by your provider<br><br>£ ⬚⬚⬚⬚⬚⬚⬚ · 0 0 | **4** Payments to an overseas pension scheme which is not UK-registered which are eligible for tax relief and were not deducted from your pay before tax<br><br>£ ⬚⬚⬚⬚⬚⬚⬚ · 0 0 |

You may need the following paperwork to find the figures required:

| | |
|---|---|
| Pension statements from the insurance company or from the trustees of your employer's scheme | |

More information and tax tips on pensions and pension contributions can be found on page 164 of this book, which also covers any pension savings tax charges and other liabilities that will need to be declared in another part of the tax return.

Most contributions to an employer's pension scheme are deducted from an employees pay and the employee is therefore getting tax relief automatically. You do not have to enter these contributions in the tax return.

**Box 1.** This covers payments you have made directly to a pension provider. These will have been made net of basic rate tax and you need to add this tax to the net amount you have actually paid to arrive at the figure to declare in your tax return. If you are entitled to higher rate tax relief then this will be adjusted in your end of year tax calculation.

**Box 2.** This covers any authorised payment you have made to a retirement annuity contract which will not have had basic rate tax deducted from the payments. Show the amount you have actually paid.

**Box 3.** If for any reason your employer was unable to deduct basic rate tax from your pension contribution then enter the amount contributed in box 3. Tax relief will be calculated and shown on your end of year tax calculation.

**Box 4.** You may be in a position where you make contributions to an overseas pension scheme, in which case basic rate tax will not have been deducted. Show the amount contributed in box 4.

## Charitable giving

| 5 Gift Aid payments made in the year to 5 April 2008 | 8 Gift Aid payments made after 5 April 2008 but to be treated as if made in the year to 5 April 2008 - *read page TRG 14 of the guide* |
| £ ⎵⎵⎵⎵⎵⎵⎵ . 0 0 | £ ⎵⎵⎵⎵⎵⎵⎵ . 0 0 |
| 6 Total of any 'one-off' payments in box 5 | |
| £ ⎵⎵⎵⎵⎵⎵⎵ . 0 0 | 9 Value of any shares or securities gifted to charity |
| | £ ⎵⎵⎵⎵⎵⎵⎵ . 0 0 |
| 7 Gift Aid payments made in the year to 5 April 2008 but treated as if made in the year to 5 April 2007 - *read page TRG 14 of the guide* | 10 Value of any land and buildings gifted to charity |
| £ ⎵⎵⎵⎵⎵⎵⎵ . 0 0 | £ ⎵⎵⎵⎵⎵⎵⎵ . 0 0 |

You may need the following paperwork in order to find the figures required:

| | |
|---|---|
| Copies of any signed covenants | |
| Records of cash donations | |
| Contract notes for shares, assets, etc. | |
| Certificates from charities confirming gifts | |

More information and tax tips on tax efficient ways of giving to charity under gift aid can be found on page 89 of this book.

You do not have to enter any sums contributed under a payroll giving scheme as you will have already had tax relief because your employer will have deducted your contribution from your pay before applying PAYE tax.

**Box 5.** This refers to *regular* gift aid payments – use the working sheet on page 179 of this book to keep a record of how you arrive at the total to go in your tax return. Enter the amounts actually paid by you. If you have previously asked that any tax repayment due to you should, instead, be paid to a charity, then you should include this amount in the total.

**Box 6.** This covers incidental gift aid payments that you may not necessarily repeat on a regular basis.

**Box 7.** If you had stated in your last tax return that you wanted payments made in the 2007–2008 tax year applied to your previous years' earning, state the amount in box 7. (Refer to page 90 of this book for guidance).

**Box 8.** Conversely, if you think it would be beneficial to you tax-wise to have any such payments made between 6 April 2008 and the date you send in your tax return applied to the 2007–2008 year, then enter such sum in box 8.

**Boxes 9 and 10.** The above boxes dealt with any cash payments you made to charity. You may have gifted shares or land or buildings, in which case enter the amounts here. Refer to page 90 for advice on how best to benefit from such contributions.

## Blind person's allowance

| 11 | If you are registered blind on a local authority or other register, put 'X' in the box | 13 | If you want your spouse's, or civil partner's, surplus allowance, put 'X' in the box |
|----|----|----|----|
| 12 | Enter the name of the local authority or other register | 14 | If you want your spouse, or civil partner, to have your surplus allowance, put 'X' in the box |

**Boxes 11 and 12.** In this section you can claim for the blind person's allowance by completing these boxes. Not all local authorities in Scotland and Northern Ireland maintain a register of blind persons. Provided you meet all the qualifications for the allowance, you should enter either 'Scottish claim' or 'Northern Ireland claim' in this section.

**Boxes 13 and 14.** If it is beneficial to transfer this allowance between partners, then put an X in either of these boxes (see page 93 for help here).

## Service companies

> 1 Total amount of any income included anywhere on this Tax
> Return, derived from the provision of your services through
> a service company - *read page TRG 15 of the guide*
>
> £ ⬚⬚⬚⬚⬚⬚⬚ . 0 0

You have to state here any income declared in your tax return that originated from a service company. This is still a very grey area of the tax legislation and is covered on page 129 of this book.

## Finishing your tax return

You will not have finished your tax return until you have completed any supplementary pages – refresh your memory by checking the summary on pages 22–23.

Do you want to calculate your own tax? If you do, you can either use the tax calculation summary pages that the tax office can supply (telephone 0845 9000 404 if you want a copy or download from **www.hmrc.gov.uk**), which are very comprehensive as they have to cover all conceivable situations and are thus necessarily complicated; or you can use the *Check Your Tax* calculator on page 170 of this book if your tax affairs are fairly straightforward.

You must send in your completed tax return by 31 October 2008, or file online, when the calculations will be done automatically, by 31 January 2009.

### Tax refunded or set-off

> 1 If you have had any 2007-08 Income Tax refunded or set-off by us or Jobcentre Plus, enter the amount
>
> £ ⬚⬚⬚⬚⬚⬚⬚ . 0 0

State the amount in **box 1** if you have received any tax refunded in respect of the 2007–2008 tax year.

### If you have not paid enough tax

Use the payslip at the foot of your next statement (or reminder) from us to pay any tax due.

> 2 If you owe tax for 2007-08 and have a PAYE tax code, we will try to collect the tax due (up to £2,000) through your tax code for 2009-10, unless you put 'X' in the box
>
> ⬚

> 3 If you are likely to owe tax for **2008-09** on income other than employed earnings or pensions, and you do **not** want us to use your 2008-09 PAYE tax code to collect that tax during the year, put 'X' in the box - *read page TRG 18 of the guide*
>
> ⬚

**Box 2.** Any underpayment of tax below £2,000 for 2007–2008 will normally be collected by an adjustment in your PAYE tax if the return is submitted by the 31 October 2008 deadline unless you put an 'X' in box 2, in which case you will have to send a cheque to HMRC when the liability is agreed.

**Box 3.** If it is likely that you will owe tax for 2008–2009 and don't want the tax office to make an allowance for this in your next PAYE code number (for example, you may not want your employer to know of the existence of other earnings) then put an 'X' in box 3.

## If you have paid too much tax or you have a tax adviser

| | |
|---|---|
| **4** Name of bank or building society | **10** If you have entered a nominee's name in box 5, put 'X' in the box |
| **5** Name of account holder (or nominee) | **11** If your nominee is your tax adviser, put 'X' in the box |
| | **12** Nominee's address |
| **6** Branch sort code | |
| **7** Account number | **13** and postcode |
| **8** Building society reference number | **14** To authorise your nominee to receive any repayment, you must sign in the box. A photocopy of your signature will not do |
| **9** If you do not have a bank or building society account, read the notes on page TRG 19 of the guide and put 'X' in the box | |
| **15** Your tax adviser's name | **17** The first line of their address and the postcode |
| **16** Their phone number | **18** The reference your adviser uses for you |

Any other information

**19** Please give any other information in this space

**Boxes 4 to 18.** Fill in all your personal bank details so that any refund can be paid directly into your bank account; similarly fill in the requested details if you have a tax adviser.

**Box 19.** Use this if you want to bring to the notice of the tax office any major change in your tax affairs.

## Signing your form and sending it back

**Box 20.** If some of the figures in your tax return are estimated, put an 'X' here. Wherever possible it is better to provide accurate figures when you send in your return as this will prevent having to correspond, perhaps extensively, with the tax office and may delay agreeing your tax liability, which may result in penalties and interest.

**Box 21.** Put an 'X' here if you are enclosing any supplementary pages (see page 22).

| 20 If this Tax Return contains provisional or estimated figures, put 'X' in the box | 21 If you are enclosing separate supplementary pages, put 'X' in the box |
|---|---|

22 If you give false information, you may have to pay financial penalties and face prosecution. Please sign and date this form.

The information I have given on this Tax Return is correct and complete to the best of my knowledge and belief

Date *DD MM YYYY*

Signature

| 23 If you have signed on behalf of someone else, enter the capacity. For example, executor, receiver | 25 If you filled in boxes 23 and 24 enter your name |
|---|---|

| 24 Enter the name of the person you have signed for | 26 and your address |
|---|---|

Finally, please send us your completed form in the envelope provided.

**Boxes 22 to 26.** Make sure that you then sign and date the declaration. A surprising number of returns are unsigned and the tax office will return them – if you are close to the filing deadline this omission could render your return 'late' and you may have to pay penalties or interest.

When you sign your tax return, you are declaring that to the best of your knowledge the return is complete, true and accurate.

It is often thought that if you keep quiet about some of your income, then the tax inspector will not find out about it. This is not the case. The tax authorities have many sources of information, the most common being your employer, banks, building societies and other businesses, all of whom may be required to make a return of payments made to individuals and businesses.

## What if you have made a mistake?

Do not worry if you have forgotten to claim an allowance due to you, for you have a time limit of five years from the relevant 31 January date after the tax year end in which to tell your tax office of your mistake and claim a refund.

If you forget to include some of your income on the form, you should immediately notify your tax office explaining your error.

## When to send in your 2008 tax return

You must send in your tax return by 31 October 2008, or if you received the form after that date then two months after the date of receipt. You have until 31 January 2009 if you file it electronically via the internet – see below.

## Filing your tax return over the internet

You can file your full tax return (but not the short version) and the supplementary pages over the internet if you find that is more convenient.

If you just use the free software package, which you can download from **www.hmrc.gov.uk**, then, apart from the main tax return (SA100), you can only file the *Employment* pages (SA102); *Self-employment* pages (SA103), *Partnership* pages (SA104) and the *UK Property* pages (SA105). However, if you need any of the other supplementary pages, you will have to file manually. Alternatively you can buy one of the many commercial software packages available and then you can file all sections of the return electronically.

The free software package will work on a PC (Windows 98 or above; Internet Explorer 5.0 or above; Netscape 4.75; Opera 6.0) or AppleMac computer (OS9 or above; Internet Explorer 5.1; Netscape 4.77).

You can telephone your tax office on the number shown on your tax return; if not, you can dial the helpline 0845 9000 444 if you have any problems.

## What paperwork will you need?

To save time whilst you are online, make sure you have to hand all the paperwork to which you may need to refer. You may need forms P60, P11D or P45 unless you are self-employed, in which case you will need your detailed accounts. Additionally you may need statements covering any interest, dividends or rents received as well as details of any pension income, benefits and casual earnings summaries. If you are going to declare capital gains or losses, then you will need full details and history of all your transactions.

## The benefits of filing electronically

The main advantages are:

- You have an extended time frame in which to file your return – until 31 January 2009 instead of 31 October 2008.

- The tax calculation is automatically done on the computer but do check it carefully before submitting in case you have typed say £5,000 of interest received instead of £500!

- You get an immediate acknowledgement of filing and repayments are faster.

- The service is safe, secure, available 24 hours a day and you can view your statement (SA300) at any time.

## How to register

To register, log on to **www.hmrc.gov.uk**.

You will need your tax reference number or national insurance number. Once you have registered you will have to wait about seven days to receive confirmation in the post of your ID and a separate unique activation PIN number. Once you have this, plus a password selected by you, you can log in and start filing. As a security precaution, don't forget to destroy the communication giving you your PIN number.

Remember to print out a hard copy of your completed tax return so you can refer to it later.

## Payments on account

If you have several sources of untaxed income or you are self-employed, it is likely that you will have to make two payments on account for each tax year. For example, for the year ended 5 April 2008 the first payment of 50 per cent of your anticipated tax bill should have been made by 31 January 2008 and the second 50 per cent on 31 July 2008; any balance due, once your tax liability is agreed, is payable on 31 January 2009, although a refund may be dealt with as soon as agreed.

It is up to you to work out how much you need to pay on account. If you believe your income will be lower than the year for which your payments on account have been calculated and you wish to alter the figure that the tax office has demanded, then ask for form SA 303 on which you can explain your reasons. If your claim to reduce is excessive and you have a liability at the end of the tax year, then interest will be payable from the original date the payments should have been made on these excess reductions.

## Surcharges and penalties

There will be an automatic penalty of £100 if your 2008 tax return is not sent in by 31 January 2009 and another £100 six months later if it is still overdue. These are reduced if the tax due is less than £200, or even cancelled if the tax due has been paid by the due date. However, a tribunal may award a penalty of up to £60 a day and, if the return is 12 months late, there is a further penalty of up to 100 per cent of the tax liability.

In addition, a surcharge may arise on any tax paid late – 5 per cent of any balancing tax due by 31 January if unpaid at 28 February, and a further 5 per cent if unpaid by 31 July (plus interest on the first surcharge).

There are also fines of up to £3,000 for each failure to keep adequate records to support figures in your tax return.

## Problems with your tax office

Contact your tax enquiry office initially if you have a query; then your tax inspector. If you still do not get satisfaction, write to the District Inspector or Regional Controller or as a last resort the Revenue and Customs adjudicator.

## Keep your records

The law requires you to keep all records of earnings, income, benefits, profits and expenses, etc. and all relevant information for 22 months from the end of the tax year and five years and ten months if you are self-employed.

If the tax office have commenced a formal enquiry into a tax return before the expiry of the time limit, the records must be kept until that enquiry is completed.

## Supplementary pages

**Having completed the main tax return (SA100) you now have to complete any supplementary pages that you ticked as 'yes' on page TR2 of your tax return.**

## Employment SA102

The supplementary pages headed *Employment* cover your income and benefits from employment and your claim for expenses. (There are different versions of this form for ministers of religion and Members of Parliament and the regional assemblies.)

After each section there is a cross-reference to the chapter or page in this book that will give you help in filling in this form.

To fill in these sections you may need copies of your:

| | |
|---|---|
| P60 or P45 forms | |
| Notice of tax code | |
| P11D form | |
| Receipts for expenses, etc. | |

These pages must be completed even if you were employed and received no income from that employer, unless that employment ceased before 6 April 2007.

---

**HM Revenue & Customs**

**Employment**

Tax year 6 April 2007 to 5 April 2008

Your name

Your unique taxpayer reference (UTR)

### Complete an *Employment* page for each employment or directorship

1 Pay from this employment - the total from your P45 or P60 - *before tax was taken off*

£ · 0 0

2 Tax taken off pay in box 1

£ · 0 0

3 Tips and other payments not on your P60 - *read page EN 3 of the notes*

£ · 0 0

4 PAYE tax reference of your employer (on your P45/P60)

5 Your employer's name

6 If you were a company director, put 'X' in the box

7 And, if the company was a close company, put 'X' in the box - *read page EN 3 of the notes*

8 If you are a part-time teacher in England and Wales and are on the Repayment of Teachers' Loans Scheme for this employment, put 'X' in the box

---

## Pay from your employer and employment details

Refer to Chapter 5 (see page 65) for more background information and advice on employment income and benefits.

**Boxes 1 and 2.** You will find the totals to go in these boxes on the P60 form your employer will have given you at the year end (see page 65); if you have left an employment, you will need to get the figure from the P45 form that your previous employer will have given you.

Any deductions made by your employer for your contributions to an approved pension scheme, payroll giving donations, or taxable lump sum leaving payment should have been deducted from the figure shown on your P60 form and only this net earnings figure should be shown in box 1 but before deducting any tax.

You do not have to include in the tax return any child tax credit or working tax credit that you may have received.

Any jobseeker's allowance included in your P60 or P45 form should not be shown here but in box 14 on page TR3 of your main tax return (see page 25).

**Box 3.** Tips and gratuities should be shown here if they are not included in your P60 form.

**Boxes 4 to 8.** Fill in the personal details.

## Benefits from your employment

| | |
|---|---|
| 9 Company cars and vans - *the total 'cash equivalent' amount* | 13 Goods and other assets provided by your employer *- the total value or amount* |
| £ · 0 0 | £ · 0 0 |
| 10 Fuel for company cars and vans - *the total 'cash equivalent' amount* | 14 Accommodation provided by your employer - *the total value or amount* |
| £ · 0 0 | £ · 0 0 |
| 11 Private medical and dental insurance - *the total 'cash equivalent' amount* | 15 Other benefits (including interest-free and low interest loans) - *the total 'cash equivalent' amount* |
| £ · 0 0 | £ · 0 0 |
| 12 Vouchers, credit cards and excess mileage allowance | 16 Expenses payments received and balancing charges |
| £ · 0 0 | £ · 0 0 |

**Boxes 9 and 10.** Company cars and vans see pages 66 and 69.

**Box 11.** See page 72.

**Box 12.** See page 69.

**Box 13.** See page 71.

**Box 14.** See page 70.

**Box 15.** See pages 70–71.

**Box 16.** See pages 73 and 125.

Note that share option schemes and share benefits and lump sum compensation paid on termination of employment have to be declared on the *Additional information* pages (see page 73).

## Employment expenses

| | |
|---|---|
| 17 Business travel and subsistence expenses | 19 Professional fees and subscriptions |
| £ · 0 0 | £ · 0 0 |
| 18 Fixed deductions for expenses | 20 Other expenses and capital allowances |
| £ · 0 0 | £ · 0 0 |

**Boxes 17 to 20.** These allow you to claim authorised expenses which you can set against your income for tax purposes. These are fully covered, with tax tips, in Chapter 6 (see page 78). Use the working sheets at the back of this book to add together the various expenses as you only have to put the total in the tax return and the tax office may ask for details at a later date.

### More than one employment

All the boxes on page E1 are repeated on page E2 in case you have, or have had, a second employment during the tax year, as you must declare income and expenses from each employment separately; you may need further copies of these sheets if you have more than two employers (for example, you are a director of several companies). Telephone 0845 9000 404 if you require further copies.

## Self-employment SA 103

These supplementary pages cover your business details. There are two types of supplementary pages ('short' and 'full'). The short version reproduced below can be used where your turnover is less than £64,000 a year (or pro-rata if you have not been trading for a full year). A separate sheet needs to be completed for each business. There is a different version for Lloyds underwriting names.

To fill in these sections you may need copies of:

| | |
|---|---|
| Financial accounts and records | |
| Previous year's tax records | |
| Details of capital expenditure | |

You must fill in these pages if you were in business on a self-employed or freelance basis, or you let furnished rooms and provided services so that it was considered as a business. If you were in partnership, you need the *Partnership* supplementary pages (see page 42). See page 26 if your freelance earnings could be considered as casual and not ongoing.

Although these supplementary pages appear very complicated at first glance, they are basically requesting the information that should be available from your business accounts but they are summarised under individual boxes for turnover and expense headings, with separate boxes for capital allowances, adjustments to profits for tax purposes and carrying forward of any losses.

Chapter 13 (see page 118) covers all basic aspects of self-employment, including those expenses that are not allowed for tax as well as deductions that you can make.

## HM Revenue & Customs

# Self-employment (short)
Tax year 6 April 2007 to 5 April 2008

**Your name**

**Your unique taxpayer reference (UTR)**

## Business details

**1** Description of business

**2** Postcode of your business address

**3** If your business name, description, address or postcode have changed in the last 12 months, put 'X' in the box and give details in the 'Any other information' box of your Tax Return

**4** If you are a foster carer or adult placement carer, put 'X' in the box – *read page SESN 2 of the notes*

**5** If your business started after 5 April 2007, enter the start date *DD MM YYYY*

**6** If your business ceased before 6 April 2008, enter the final date of trading

**7** Date your books or accounts are made up to – *read page SESN 2 of the notes*

## Business income – if your annual business turnover was below £64,000

**8** Your turnover – *the takings, fees, sales or money earned by your business*

£ . 0 0

**9** Any other business income not included in box 8 – *excluding Business Start-up allowance*

£ . 0 0

## Allowable business expenses

Read page SESN 3 of the *notes* to see which expenses are allowable for tax purposes. If your annual turnover was below £30,000 you may just put your total expenses in box 19, rather than filling in the whole section.

**10** Costs of goods bought for re-sale or goods used

£ . 0 0

**11** Car, van and travel expenses – *after private use proportion*

£ . 0 0

**12** Wages, salaries and other staff costs

£ . 0 0

**13** Rent, rates, power and insurance costs

£ . 0 0

**14** Repairs and renewals of property and equipment

£ . 0 0

**15** Accountancy, legal and other professional fees

£ . 0 0

**16** Interest and bank and credit card etc. financial charges

£ . 0 0

**17** Telephone, fax, stationery and other office costs

£ . 0 0

**18** Other allowable business expenses – *client entertaining costs are not an allowable expense*

£ . 0 0

**19** Total allowable expenses – *total of boxes 10 to 18*

£ . 0 0

## Net profit or loss

**20** Net profit - *if your business income is more than your expenses (box 8 + box 9 minus box 19)*

£ _____ . 0 0

**21** Or, net loss - *if your expenses exceed your business income (box 8 + box 9 minus box 19 is negative)*

£ _____ . 0 0

## Tax allowances for vehicles and equipment (capital allowances)

There are 'capital' tax allowances for vehicles and equipment used in your business (you should not have included the cost of these in your business expenses). Read pages SESN 3 to SESN 6 of the *notes* and use the example and Working Sheets to work out your capital allowances.

**22** Total capital allowances

£ _____ . 0 0

**23** Total balancing charges - where you have disposed of items for more than their value - *read page SESN 4 of the notes*

£ _____ . 0 0

# Boxes 22 and 23. Refer to page 126 and 125.

## Calculating your taxable profits

Your taxable profit may not be the same as your net profit. Read page SESN 7 of the *notes* to see if you need to make any adjustments and fill in the boxes which apply to arrive at your taxable profit for the year.

**24** Goods or services for your own use - *read page SESN 7 of the notes*

£ _____ . 0 0

**26** Loss brought forward from earlier years set-off against this year's profits - *up to the amount in box 25*

£ _____ . 0 0

**25** Net business profit for tax purposes (box 20 or box 21 + box 23 + box 24 minus box 22)

£ _____ . 0 0

**27** Any other business income not included in boxes 8 or 9 - *for example, Business Start-up Allowance*

£ _____ . 0 0

## Total taxable profits or net business loss

**28** Total taxable profits from this business (box 25 + box 27 minus box 26)

£ _____ . 0 0

**29** Net business loss for tax purposes (if box 20 or box 21 + box 23 + box 24 minus box 22 is negative)

£ _____ . 0 0

## Losses, Class 4 NICs and deductions

If you have made a loss for tax purposes (box 29), read page SESN 7 of the *notes* and fill in boxes 30 to 32 as appropriate

**30** Loss from this tax year set-off against other income for 2007-08

£ _____ . 0 0

**33** If you are exempt from paying Class 4 NICs, put 'X' in the box - *read page SESN 8 of the notes*

□

**31** Loss to be carried back to previous year(s) and set-off against income (or capital gains)

£ _____ . 0 0

**34** If you have been given a 2007-08 Class 4 NICs deferment certificate, put 'X' in the box - *read page SESN 8 of the notes*

□

**32** Total loss to carry forward after all other set-offs - *including unused losses brought forward*

£ _____ . 0 0

**35** Deductions on payment and deduction statements from contractors - *construction industry subcontractors only*

£ _____ . 0 0

## Partnership SA104

All the background information needed to complete these pages is similar to that covered by the *Self-employment* section (see page 39) and Chapter 13 (see page 118) covers most of the basic aspects.

To fill in these sections you may need copies of:

| | |
|---|---|
| Partnership statements and accounts | |
| Previous tax records | |
| Details of capital expenditure | |

There are two types of supplementary pages: *Partnership* (short version) reproduced here and *Partnership* (full version). Use the short version if your only partnership income was trading income or taxed interest from banks, building societies or deposit takers. This will apply to the majority of small partnerships.

---

**HM Revenue & Customs**

**Partnership (short)**

Tax year 6 April 2007 to 5 April 2008

Your name

Your unique taxpayer reference (UTR)

**Complete a *Partnership* page for each partnership of which you were a member and for each business**

Partnership details

1 Partnership reference number

2 Description of partnership trade or profession

3 If you became a partner after 5 April 2007, enter the date you joined the partnership *DD MM YYYY*

4 If you left the partnership before 6 April 2008, enter the date you left

**Your share of the partnership's trading or professional profits**

If you need help, look up the box numbers in the *notes*. If you want to enter a loss, or an adjustment needs to be taken off, put a minus sign (-) in the box next to the £ sign.

5 Date your basis period began

6 Date your basis period ended

7 Your share of the partnership's profit or loss - *from box 11 or 12 on the Partnership Statement*
£ · 0 0

8 If your basis period is not the same as the partnership's accounting period, enter the adjustment needed to arrive at the profit or loss for your basis period
£ · 0 0

12 Overlap relief used this year
£ · 0 0

13 Overlap profit carried forward
£ · 0 0

14 Adjusted profit for 2007-08 (from box G of the Working Sheet on page SPN 4 of the *notes*) - *if this is a loss put '0' in this box and enter the amount of the loss in box 19*
£ · 0 0

15 Losses brought forward from earlier years set-off against this year's profit (up to the amount in box 14)
£ · 0 0

---

**9** Adjustment for change of accounting practice – *from box 11A on the Partnership Statement*

£ ⬚ . 0 0

**16** Taxable profits after losses brought forward (box 14 minus box 15)

£ ⬚ . 0 0

**10** Averaging adjustment – *only for farmers, market gardeners and creators of literary or artistic works*

£ ⬚ . 0 0

**17** Any other business income not included in the partnership accounts

£ ⬚ . 0 0

**11** Foreign tax claimed as a deduction – *only if foreign tax credit relief has not been claimed on Foreign pages*

£ ⬚ . 0 0

**18** Your share of total taxable profits from the partnership's business for 2007-08 (box 16 + box 17)

£ ⬚ . 0 0

## Your share of the partnership's trading or professional losses

**19** Adjusted loss for 2007-08 (from box H of the Working Sheet on page SPN 4 of the *notes*) – *if this is a negative*

£ ⬚ . 0 0

**21** Loss to be carried back to previous year(s) and set-off against income (or capital gains)

£ ⬚ . 0 0

**20** Loss from this tax year set-off against other income for 2007-08

£ ⬚ . 0 0

**22** Total loss to carry forward after all other set-offs – *including unused losses brought forward*

£ ⬚ . 0 0

## Class 4 National Insurance contributions (NICs)

**23** If you are exempt from paying Class 4 NICs, put 'X' in the box – *read page SPN 6 of the notes*

⬚

**25** Adjustment to profits chargeable to Class 4 NICs – *this will not apply to most people*

£ ⬚ . 0 0

**24** If you have been given a 2007-08 Class 4 NICs deferment certificate, put 'X' in the box – *read page SPN 7 of the notes*

⬚

## Your share of the partnership taxed interest etc.

**26** Your share of taxed interest etc. – *from box 22 on the Partnership Statement*

£ ⬚ . 0 0

## Your share of the partnership tax paid and deductions

**27** Your share of Income Tax taken off partnership income – *from box 25 on the Partnership Statement*

£ ⬚ . 0 0

**29** Your share of any tax taken off trading income (not contractor deductions) – *from box 24A on the Partnership Statement*

£ ⬚ . 0 0

**28** Your share of CIS deductions made by contractors – *from box 24 on the Partnership Statement*

£ ⬚ . 0 0

## Any other information

**30** Please give any other information in this space

## UK property SA105

The supplementary pages headed *UK property* cover all types of UK rental income, whether it is from numerous properties or a single rental, holiday lettings, or qualifies for rent-a-room relief.

Any income from land or property overseas should not be included here but in the *Foreign* supplementary pages and if you are running a business or trade (such as a guest house), use the *Self-employed* supplementary pages.

Page 84 of this book gives you background details regarding the taxation of land and property, joint holdings and expenses payments you might be able to claim.

**Box 4.** If you are only claiming rent-a-room relief for gross rents of £4,250 or less a year put a cross in box 4 and/or fill in box 35 (see page 85).

To fill in these pages of the tax return you may need:

| | |
|---|---|
| Records of rent received | |
| Records of expenses and bills for them | |

---

**HM Revenue & Customs**

**UK property**
Tax year 6 April 2007 to 5 April 2008

Your name

Your unique taxpayer reference (UTR)

UK property details

1 Number of properties rented out

2 If all property income ceased in 2007–08 and you do not expect to receive such income in 2008–09, put 'X' in the box

3 If you have any income from property let jointly, put 'X' in the box

4 If you are claiming Rent a Room relief and your rents are £4,250 or less (or £2,125 if let jointly), put 'X' in the box

---

## Furnished holiday lettings

Please read pages UKPN 2 to UKPN 5 of the *notes* if you have furnished holiday lettings.

**5** Income – *the amount of rent and any income for services provided to tenants*

£ ☐☐☐☐☐☐☐ . 0 0

**6** Rent paid, repairs, insurance and costs of services provided – *the total amount*

£ ☐☐☐☐☐☐☐ . 0 0

**7** Loan interest and other financial costs

£ ☐☐☐☐☐☐☐ . 0 0

**8** Legal, management and other professional fees

£ ☐☐☐☐☐☐☐ . 0 0

**9** Other allowable property expenses

£ ☐☐☐☐☐☐☐ . 0 0

**10** Private use adjustment – *if expenses include any amounts for non-business purposes*

£ ☐☐☐☐☐☐☐ . 0 0

**11** Balancing charges – *read page UKPN 4 of the notes*

£ ☐☐☐☐☐☐☐ . 0 0

**12** Capital allowances – *read page UKPN 4 of the notes*

£ ☐☐☐☐☐☐☐ . 0 0

**13** Profit for the year (box 5 + box 10 + box 11 minus (boxes 6 to 9 + box 12))

£ ☐☐☐☐☐☐☐ . 0 0

## Furnished holiday lettings losses

Please read pages UKPN 5 and UKPN 6 of the *notes* before filling in boxes 15 to 17.

**14** Loss for the year (box 5 + box 10 + box 11 minus (boxes 6 to 9 + box 12))

£ ☐☐☐☐☐☐☐ . 0 0

**15** Loss set-off against other income from property

£ ☐☐☐☐☐☐☐ . 0 0

**16** Loss set-off against 2007-08 total income

£ ☐☐☐☐☐☐☐ . 0 0

**17** Loss carried back to earlier years

£ ☐☐☐☐☐☐☐ . 0 0

## Property income

Do not include Real Estate Investment Trust dividends/distributions here.

**18** Total rents and other income from property (including any furnished holiday lettings profits in box 13)

£ ☐☐☐☐☐☐☐ . 0 0

**19** Tax taken off any income in box 18

£ ☐☐☐☐☐☐☐ . 0 0

**20** Premiums for the grant of a lease - *from box E on the Working Sheet on page UKPN 7 of the notes.*

£ ☐☐☐☐☐☐☐ . 0 0

**21** Reverse premiums and inducements

£ ☐☐☐☐☐☐☐ . 0 0

## Property expenses

**22** Rent, rates, insurance, ground rents, etc.

£ ☐☐☐☐☐☐☐ . 0 0

**23** Property repairs, maintenance and renewals

£ ☐☐☐☐☐☐☐ . 0 0

**24** Loan interest and other financial costs

£ ☐☐☐☐☐☐☐ . 0 0

**25** Legal, management and other professional fees

£ ☐☐☐☐☐☐☐ . 0 0

**26** Costs of services provided, including wages

£ ☐☐☐☐☐☐☐ . 0 0

**27** Other allowable property expenses

£ ☐☐☐☐☐☐☐ . 0 0

## Calculating your taxable profit or loss

**28** Private use adjustment – *read page UKPN 8 of the notes*

£ ⬚⬚⬚⬚⬚⬚⬚ . 0 0

**29** Balancing charges – *read page UKPN 9 of the notes*

£ ⬚⬚⬚⬚⬚⬚⬚ . 0 0

**30** Capital allowances for equipment, vehicles and some types of buildings – *read page UKPN 9 of the notes*

£ ⬚⬚⬚⬚⬚⬚⬚ . 0 0

**31** Business Premises Renovation Allowance (Assisted Areas only) – *read pages UKPN 9 and 10 of the notes*

£ ⬚⬚⬚⬚⬚⬚⬚ . 0 0

**32** Enhanced capital allowances at 100% – *read page UKPN 10 of the notes*

£ ⬚⬚⬚⬚⬚⬚⬚ . 0 0

**33** Landlord's Energy Saving Allowance – *read page UKPN 10 of the notes*

£ ⬚⬚⬚⬚⬚⬚⬚ . 0 0

**34** 10% wear and tear allowance – *for furnished residential accommodation only. Read page UKPN 10 of the notes*

£ ⬚⬚⬚⬚⬚⬚⬚ . 0 0

**35** Rent a Room exempt amount – *read page UKPN 10 of the notes*

£ ⬚⬚⬚⬚ . 0 0

**36** Adjusted profit for the year – *from box O on the Working Sheet on page UKPN 11*

£ ⬚⬚⬚⬚⬚⬚⬚ . 0 0

**37** Loss brought forward from previous year

£ ⬚⬚⬚⬚⬚⬚⬚ . 0 0

**38** Taxable profit for the year (box 36 minus box 37)

£ ⬚⬚⬚⬚⬚⬚⬚ . 0 0

**39** Adjusted loss for the year – *from box O on the Working Sheet on page UKPN 11*

£ ⬚⬚⬚⬚⬚⬚⬚ . 0 0

**40** Loss set-off against 2007–08 total income – *this will be unusual*

£ ⬚⬚⬚⬚⬚⬚⬚ . 0 0

**41** Loss to carry forward to following year, including unused losses brought forward

£ ⬚⬚⬚⬚⬚⬚⬚ . 0 0

## Foreign SA106

The supplementary pages headed *Foreign* cover all savings or property income, pensions and benefits that you receive from abroad.

To fill in these sections of the tax return you may need:

| | |
|---|---|
| Business accounts and records | |
| Pension and social security advice notes | |
| Dividend and interest statements | |
| Property records and rents received records | |
| Contract notes for investment transactions | |
| Foreign tax payment details | |

Do not declare earnings from work done abroad in this section. These must be declared in either the *Employment, Self-employment* or *Partnership* supplementary pages.

If you have made capital gaines or losses, then these should be declared on the *Capital gains* supplementary pages, although any foreign tax incurred should be stated here.

Tax rules and regulations concerning foreign income are particularly complex – you will need to refer to the extensive notes that come with the tax return. See in particular page 76 of this book.

---

**HM Revenue & Customs**

**Foreign**

Tax year 6 April 2007 to 5 April 2008

**Remittance basis**

1 If you are making a claim for the remittance basis, put 'X' in the box - *read page FN 2 of the notes*

☐

**Unremittable income**

2 If you were unable to transfer any of your overseas income to the UK, put 'X' in the box - *read page FN 3 of the notes and give details in the 'Any other information' box on your Tax Return or on a separate schedule*

☐

**Foreign tax credit relief**

If foreign tax was taken off your foreign income you may be able to claim foreign tax credit relief. Read pages FN 3 and FN 4 of the *notes* to see if you can claim the relief and how you should make the claim.

If you are calculating your tax bill you may also want to calculate your foreign tax credit relief. If you do, use the Working Sheet provided in Help Sheet 263 *Foreign tax credit relief* and fill in box 3.

3 If you are calculating your tax, enter the total foreign tax credit relief on your income

£ ☐☐☐☐☐☐☐☐

---

A Country or territory code    B Amount of income arising or received    C Foreign tax taken off or paid
                               before any tax taken off

Interest and other income from overseas savings

Dividends from foreign companies

Overseas pensions, social security benefits and royalties etc.

Dividend income received by an overseas trust; company or other person abroad (if you are omitting income from this section because you are claiming an exemption, see box 46)

All other income received by an overseas trust; company or other person abroad (if you are omitting income from this section because you are claiming an exemption, see box 46)

D Special Withholding Tax and any    E To claim foreign tax    F Taxable amount – *if you are claiming*
  UK tax taken off                     credit relief put 'X' in    *foreign tax credit relief, copy column B*
                                       the box                     *here. If not, enter column B minus column C*

## Income from land and property abroad
## Income and expenses

**14** Total rents and other receipts (excluding taxable premiums for the grant of a lease)

£ ⬚⬚⬚⬚⬚⬚⬚⬚⬚

**15** If box 14 contains income from more than one property, enter the number of properties

⬚⬚

**16** Premiums paid for the grant of a lease - *from box E on the Working Sheet*

£ ⬚⬚⬚⬚⬚⬚⬚⬚⬚

**17** Property expenses (rent, repairs, legal fees, cost of services provided) - *enter the total amount*

£ ⬚⬚⬚⬚⬚⬚⬚⬚⬚

**18** Net profit or loss (box 14 + box 16 minus box 17) - *if this is a negative figure (a loss) put a minus sign in the box*

£ ⬚⬚⬚⬚⬚⬚⬚⬚⬚

## Summary
If you have filled in any of boxes 14 to 24 enter the details below.

| A Country or territory code | B Adjusted profit or loss (from box 24) | C Foreign tax taken off or paid |
|---|---|---|
| ⬚⬚⬚ | £ ⬚⬚⬚⬚⬚⬚⬚⬚⬚ | £ ⬚⬚⬚⬚⬚⬚⬚⬚ |
| ⬚⬚⬚ | £ ⬚⬚⬚⬚⬚⬚⬚⬚⬚ | £ ⬚⬚⬚⬚⬚⬚⬚⬚ |
| ⬚⬚⬚ | £ ⬚⬚⬚⬚⬚⬚⬚⬚⬚ | £ ⬚⬚⬚⬚⬚⬚⬚⬚ |

**25** Total of column above

£ ⬚⬚⬚⬚⬚⬚⬚⬚⬚

**26** Loss brought forward from earlier years

£ ⬚⬚⬚⬚⬚⬚⬚⬚⬚

**27** Total taxable profits (box 25 minus box 26 - *if this is a positive amount*)

£ ⬚⬚⬚⬚⬚⬚⬚⬚⬚

**28** Total foreign tax

£ ⬚⬚⬚⬚⬚⬚⬚⬚

**Losses**

**31** Loss offset against total income

£ ⬚⬚⬚⬚⬚⬚⬚⬚⬚

**32** Loss to carry forward to the following year (box 25 minus box 26 + box 31)

£ ⬚⬚⬚⬚⬚⬚⬚⬚⬚

## Calculating profits and losses for tax purposes

**19** Private use adjustment - *read page FN 11 of the notes*

£ ⬚⬚⬚⬚⬚⬚⬚⬚⬚

**20** Balancing charges - *read page FN 11 of the notes*

£ ⬚⬚⬚⬚⬚⬚⬚⬚⬚

**21** Capital allowances for equipment and vehicles (but not for furnished residential lettings)

£ ⬚⬚⬚⬚⬚⬚⬚⬚⬚

**22** Landlord's energy saving allowance

£ ⬚⬚⬚⬚⬚⬚⬚⬚⬚

**23** 10% wear and tear allowance (for furnished residential lettings only)

£ ⬚⬚⬚⬚⬚⬚⬚⬚⬚

**24** Adjusted profit or loss for the year (box 18 + box 19 + box 20 minus (boxes 21 to 23))

£ ⬚⬚⬚⬚⬚⬚⬚⬚⬚

| D UK tax taken off | E To claim foreign tax credit relief put 'X' in the box | F Taxable amount - *see note on page FN 13* |
|---|---|---|
| £ ⬚⬚⬚⬚⬚⬚⬚⬚ | ⬚ | £ ⬚⬚⬚⬚⬚⬚⬚⬚ |

## Foreign tax paid on employment, self-employment and other income

If you are claiming foreign tax credit relief on income included elsewhere in your Tax Return, fill in the columns below and say in the 'Any other information' box (on page TR 6) where on your Tax Return this income is included. The country or territory codes are on pages FN 17 to FN 19 of the *notes*.

| A Country or territory code | C Foreign tax paid | E To claim foreign tax credit relief put 'X' in the box | F Taxable amount – *see note on page FN 14* |
|---|---|---|---|
| ☐☐☐ | £ | ☐ | £ |
| ☐☐☐ | £ | ☐ | £ |
| ☐☐☐ | £ | ☐ | £ |
| ☐☐☐ | £ | ☐ | £ |

## Capital gains - foreign tax credit relief and Special Withholding Tax

If you have completed *Capital Gains Summary* pages and you have paid foreign tax on those gains, and you want to claim foreign tax credit relief for the foreign tax, fill in boxes 33 to 40 below.

**33** Amount of chargeable gain under UK rules
£

**37** Foreign tax paid
£

**34** Number of days over which UK gain accrued
☐☐☐

**38** To claim foreign tax credit relief, put 'X' in the box
☐

**35** Amount of chargeable gain under foreign tax rules
£

**39** Total foreign tax credit relief on gains
£

**36** Number of days over which foreign gain accrued
☐☐☐

**40** Special Withholding Tax
£

## Other overseas income and gains

**41** Gains on disposals of holdings in offshore funds (excluding the amounts entered in box 13) and discretionary income from non-resident trusts - *enter the amount of the gain or payment*
£

**44** Number of years
☐☐

**45** Tax treated as paid - *read page FN 16 of the notes*
£

**42** If you have received a benefit from an overseas trust; company or other person abroad, enter the value or payment received - *read page FN 15 of the notes*
£

**46** If you have omitted income from boxes 11, 13 and 42 because you are claiming an exemption in relation to a transfer of assets, enter the total amount omitted (and give full details in the 'Any other information' box)
£

**43** Gains on foreign life insurance policies etc. (excluding the amounts entered in box 13) - *enter the amount of the gain*
£

## Trusts, etc. SA107

The supplementary pages headed *Trusts etc.* enable you to declare any income you receive from trusts, settlements or estates of deceased persons.

To fill in these sections you may need:

| | |
|---|---|
| Dividend and interest statements from the trustees or personal representatives (form R185 in particular) | |
| Correspondence identifying the type of trust, etc. | |

Tax deducted from such income may be at varying tax rates and you need to identify these in the relevant boxes of the tax return. The trustees will identify the type of tax rate that has been applied.

See also page 86 for further background information.

---

**HM Revenue & Customs**

**Trusts etc.**

Tax year 6 April 2007 to 5 April 2008

Your name

Your unique taxpayer reference (UTR)

**Income from trusts and settlements**

Discretionary income payment from a trust

1 Net amount - *after tax taken off*
£ · 0 0

2 Total payments from settlor-interested trusts
£ · 0 0

Non-discretionary income entitlement from a trust

3 Net amount taxed at basic rate - *after tax taken off*
£ · 0 0

5 Net amount taxed at dividend rate - *after tax taken off*
£ · 0 0

4 Net amount taxed at savings rate - *after tax taken off*
£ · 0 0

6 If you have included income from trusts or settlements whose trustees are not resident in the UK for tax purposes, put 'X' in the box

---

## Income chargeable on settlors

Read pages TN 2 and TN 3 of the *Trusts etc. notes* and complete these boxes.

**7** Net amount taxed at basic rate – *after tax taken off*

£ · 0 0

**8** Net amount taxed at savings rate – *after tax taken off*

£ · 0 0

**9** Net amount taxed at dividend rate – *after tax taken off*

£ · 0 0

**10** Net amount taxed at trust rate – *after tax taken off*

£ · 0 0

**11** Net amount taxed at dividend trust rate – *after tax taken off*

£ · 0 0

**12** Gross income – *to be taxed at basic rate*

£ · 0 0

**13** Gross income – *to be taxed at savings rate*

£ · 0 0

**14** Additional tax paid by the trustees on certain UK life insurance policy etc. gains – *read page TN 2 of the notes*

£ · 0 0

## Income from the estates of deceased persons

### Income from UK estates

**15** Income taxed at basic rate – *after tax taken off*

£ · 0 0

**16** Income taxed at savings rate – *after tax taken off*

£ · 0 0

**17** Income taxed at dividend rate – *after tax taken off*

£ · 0 0

**18** Income taxed at non-repayable basic rate – *after tax taken off*

£ · 0 0

**19** Income taxed at non-repayable savings rate – *after tax taken off*

£ · 0 0

**20** Income taxed at non-payable dividend rate – *after tax taken off*

£ · 0 0

### Income from foreign estates

**21** Foreign estate income

£ · 0 0

**22** Relief for UK tax already accounted for

£ · 0 0

## Foreign tax paid on estate income

**23** Foreign tax for which foreign tax credit relief has not been claimed

£ · 0 0

## Any other information

**24** Please give any other information in this space

## Capital gains summary SA108

The supplementary pages headed *Capital gains* cover all capital gains and losses on all assets in the UK and overseas.

You have to fill in these sheets if you sold or gave away assets worth more than £36,800 and/or your net chargeable gains for tax purposes after the deduction of current year losses were £9,200 or more in the year ended 5 April 2008 or you want to claim a capital loss or make any other election.

To complete this section of the return you will need:

| | |
|---|---|
| Copies of contract notes for the sale and purchase of shares | |
| Invoices and letters about the purchase and sale of other assets | |
| Invoices for all allowable expenses you can claim | |

Chapter 15 (see page 134) covers all aspects of capital gains.

When you receive the capital gains pages there will be attached capital gains summary notes and help sheets. If you have only a few transactions, this section of the tax return need not be too difficult to complete and you may well be under the parameters mentioned above. If you have a great number of transactions it may well be wise to get professional help. It is almost unbelievable just how complicated capital gains tax has become over the last few years, although the abolition of tapering relief and the introduction of a flat rate of capital gains tax may reduce the problems when you come to fill in your 2009 tax return.

**HM Revenue & Customs**

# Capital Gains Summary

Tax year 6 April 2007 to 5 April 2008

**1** Your name

**2** Your unique taxpayer reference (UTR)

## Summary of your enclosed computations

You **must** enclose your computations, as well as filling in the boxes.

**3** Total gains in the year, before losses and taper relief

£ · 0 0

**4** Total losses of the year

£ · 0 0

**5** Losses brought forward and used in the year

£ · 0 0

**6** Total gains, after losses and taper relief but before the annual exempt amount

£ · 0 0

**7** Annual exempt amount

£ 9 2 0 0 · 0 0

**8** Net chargeable gains (box 6 minus box 7) – but if box 7 is more than box 6, leave blank

£ · 0 0

**9** Additional liability in respect of non-resident or dual resident trusts

£ · 0 0

**10** Losses available to be carried forward to later years

£ · 0 0

**11** Losses used against an earlier year's gain (special circumstances apply – *read pages CGN6 and 11 of the Notes*)

£ · 0 0

**12** Losses used against income – *amount claimed against 2007-08 income*

£ · 0 0

**13** Losses used against income – *amount claimed against 2006-07 income*

£ · 0 0

**14** Income losses of 2007-08 set against gains

£ · 0 0

**15** If business taper relief has been applied to a gain on any asset, put 'X' in the box

## Listed shares and securities

**16** Number of disposals

**17** Disposal proceeds

£ · 0 0

**18** Allowable costs (including purchase price), and indexation

£ · 0 0

**19** Gains in the year, before losses and taper relief

£ · 0 0

**20** If you are making any claim or election, put 'X' in the box

**21** If your computations include any estimates or valuations, put 'X' in the box

## Unlisted shares and securities

**22** Number of disposals

**23** Disposal proceeds

£ ⬚⬚⬚⬚⬚⬚⬚ · 0 0

**24** Allowable costs (including purchase price), and indexation

£ ⬚⬚⬚⬚⬚⬚⬚ · 0 0

**25** Gains in the year, before losses and taper relief

£ ⬚⬚⬚⬚⬚⬚⬚ · 0 0

**26** If you are making any claim or election, put 'X' in the box

**27** If your computations include any estimates or valuations, put 'X' in the box

## Property and other assets and gains

**28** Number of disposals

**29** Disposal proceeds

£ ⬚⬚⬚⬚⬚⬚⬚ · 0 0

**30** Allowable costs (including purchase price), and indexation

£ ⬚⬚⬚⬚⬚⬚⬚ · 0 0

**31** Gains in the year, before losses and taper relief

£ ⬚⬚⬚⬚⬚⬚⬚ · 0 0

**32** Attributed gains where personal losses cannot be set-off

£ ⬚⬚⬚⬚⬚⬚⬚ · 0 0

**33** If you are making any claim or election, put 'X' in the box

**34** If your computations include any estimates or valuations, put 'X' in the box

## Any other information

**35** Please give any other information in this space

## Non residence, etc. SA109

These supplementary pages contain a sequence of questions to enable the tax office to determine or confirm your status as regards residence and domicile.

The rules governing the legal status of a person and the consequent tax implications are among some of the most difficult in our tax legislation and are outside the scope of this basic tax guide.

However, if you have requested these supplementary pages, the tax office will automatically send you a set of extensive notes and flowcharts to help you decide your tax status. If these have not been sent to you, ask your tax office for leaflet IR211 or download it from the internet from **www.hmrc.gov.uk**.

Remember that you are not liable to UK tax if you go abroad to work or live for a period which will span a complete tax year providing you curtail your trips back to the UK and they do not amount to 183 days or more per year, and are less than an average of 91 days a year for four consecutive tax years.

A new annual tax charge of £30,000 will be payable by non-domiciled residents who had been in Britain for more than seven years and wish to keep their overseas income and gains out of the UK tax net. This charge commences with the 2008–2009 tax year.

**HM Revenue & Customs**

# Non residence etc.

Tax year 6 April 2007 to 5 April 2008

Your name

Your unique taxpayer reference (UTR)

## Residence status

Work through pages NRN 1 to NRN 10 of the *notes* before you fill in boxes 1 to 9.

**1** If you were not resident in the UK for 2007-08, put 'X' in the box

**2** If you were not ordinarily resident in the UK for 2007-08, put 'X' in the box

**3** If you are requesting split-year treatment for 2007-08, put 'X' in the box

**4** If you were resident in the UK for 2006-07, put 'X' in the box

**5** If you were ordinarily resident in the UK for 2006-07, put 'X' in the box

**6** If you arrived in the UK on or after 6 April 2007, enter the date you arrived *DD MM YYYY*

**7** If you left the UK on or after 6 April 2007, enter the date you left

**8** If you work full-time abroad, or if you worked full-time abroad before the date in box 6 or after the date in box 7, put 'X' in the box

**9** If you have come to the UK to live or to remain here for an extended period, put 'X' in the box

## Time spent in the UK (if you were not resident or not ordinarily resident in the UK)

Please complete the boxes for the whole year unless you are requesting split-year treatment. If you are (you put 'X' in box 3) complete the boxes either for the period from 6 April 2007 until your arrival, or for the period from your departure until 5 April 2008.

**10** Number of days spent in the UK during 2007-08 (excluding days of arrival and departure)

**11** Number of days in box 10 attributed to exceptional circumstances

**12** Number of separate occasions that you have been to the UK during 2007-08

**13** Number of workdays you spent in the UK

**14** Number of days you have spent in the UK since 5 April 2004 or, if you left the UK after 5 April 2004, the number of days spent in the UK since you left (excluding days of arrival and departure)

## Personal allowances

**15** If you are entitled to claim personal allowances as a non-resident because of the terms of a Double Taxation Agreement, put 'X' in the box

**16** If you are entitled to claim personal allowances as a non-resident on some other basis, put 'X' in the box

**17** Enter the code(s) for the country or countries of which you are a national and/or resident – *read pages NRN 14 to NRN 16 of the notes*

## Residence in other countries and Double Taxation Relief

If you are claiming relief in box 20 or box 21, fill in the appropriate claim form in Help Sheet 302 or 304 and send this as well.

**18** Enter the code(s) for the country or countries, other than the UK, in which you were resident for tax purposes for 2007-08

**19** If you were also resident in either or both of the countries above for 2006-07, enter the appropriate code(s)

**20** Relief under Double Taxation Agreements between the UK and other countries – *amount claimed because of an agreement awarding residence to another country (see Help Sheet 302)*

£ . 0 0

**21** Relief claimed because of other provisions of the relevant Double Taxation Agreements *(see Help Sheet 304)*

£ . 0 0

## Domicile

**22** If you are domiciled outside the UK and it is relevant to your Income Tax or Capital Gains Tax liability, put 'X' in the box

**23** If 2007-08 is the first year that you have said that your domicile is outside the UK, put 'X' in the box

**24** If you have put 'X' in box 22 and have a domicile of origin within the UK, enter the date on which your domicile changed

**25** If you were born in the UK but have never been domiciled here, put 'X' in the box

**26** If you have put 'X' in box 22 and you were born outside the UK, enter the date that you came to live in the UK

## Any other information

**27** Please give any other information in this space

---

### Additional information SA101

These additional pages enclosed with your tax return cover types of income, deductions and reliefs that are less common.

## Other UK income

## Interest from gilt-edged and other UK securities

| 1 Gilt etc. interest after tax taken off | 3 Gross amount before tax |
|---|---|
| £ · 0 0 | £ · 0 0 |
| 2 Tax taken off | |
| £ · 0 0 | |

You would have expected this interest to be declared under the interest and dividends section of the main tax return, but this year it appears on these pages.

**Boxes 1 and 2.** If you have had tax deducted from the interest, then fill in the amount actually received in box 1 and the tax deducted in box 2.

**Box 3.** You can elect to have interest paid without having tax deducted on Government stocks, in which case enter the total in box 3.

Use the working sheets on page 173 of this book to keep a record of the amounts. These boxes also accommodate any profit arising from buying and selling interest-bearing securities cum dividend or ex dividend (known as accrued income profits) – you may need to refer to the notes accompanying the supplementary pages (AiN 2) as this is a complicated subject. Also refer to page 84 of this book.

## Life insurance gains

| 4 UK life insurance policy etc. gains on which tax was treated as paid - *the amount of the gain* | 8 UK life insurance policy etc. gains from voided ISAs |
|---|---|
| £ · 0 0 | £ · 0 0 |
| 5 Number of years the policy has been held or since the last gain - *whichever is less* | 9 Number of years the policy was held |
| | 10 Tax taken off box 8 |
| 6 UK life insurance policy etc. gains where no tax was treated as paid - *the amount of the gain* | £ · 0 0 |
| £ · 0 0 | 11 Deficiency relief |
| 7 Number of years the policy has been held or since the last gain - *whichever is less* | £ · 0 0 |

**Boxes 4 to 11.** Sometimes a taxable gain arises on a life insurance policy which is a non-qualifying policy. Your insurance company will have told you if this is the case and will have given you a 'chargeable event' certificate and this will show the details that you need to fill in here.

## Stock dividends, non-qualifying distributions and loans written off

| 12 | Stock dividends - the appropriate amount in cash/cash equivalent of the share capital - *without any tax* | 13 | Non-qualifying distributions and close company loans written off or released |
|---|---|---|---|
| £ ⋅ 0 0 | | £ ⋅ 0 0 | |

**Box 12.** This relates to stock dividends – these are offers of shares taken up instead of receiving a cash dividend. You will have received a dividend statement to this effect from the company involved and this is the amount you need to declare in this box.

**Box 13.** This is for non-qualifying dividends that you may have received – effectively a payment made instead of a dividend that is regarded by the tax office as being taxable. Again, you will have received a statement from the company paying the dividend to this effect. If you have received a loan from a close company and it has been written off. then this 'benefit' is taxable and should be included in box 13.

## Business receipts taxed as income of an earlier year

| 14 | The amount of post-cessation or other business receipts | 15 | Tax year income to be taxed, for example 2006-07 *YYYY YY* |
|---|---|---|---|
| £ ⋅ 0 0 | | – | |

**Box 14.** There may be circumstances where you received some late income relating to a business that had previously ceased, and which, had it been received whilst the business was still trading would have been taxable. Box 14 enables you to declare such post-cessation receipts.

**Box 15.** State the year to which it would have originally related.

## Share schemes and employment lump sums, compensation and deductions

### Share schemes
**Boxes 1 and 2.** In previous years there were supplementary pages specifically for share schemes but now you have to declare any taxable amount in these 'additional information sheets' here.

The general background information on share schemes is given on pages 73–75 of this book. However, the rules and regulations vary from scheme to scheme and they can be very complex, as will be seen from the working notes (AiN 5–AiN 24) accompanying your tax return. You must use a separate set of sheets for each share scheme.

It is important that you consult your employer or the trustees of your scheme if you require help or clarification before filling in this section of the tax return.

| 1 | Share schemes - the taxable amount - *excluding amounts included on your P60 or P45* |
| £ _____ . 0 0 |

| 2 | Tax taken off box 1 |
| £ _____ . 0 0 |

| 3 | Taxable lump sums - excluding redundancy and compensation for loss of your job - *see notes starting on page Ain 24 and Working Sheet 22* |
| £ _____ . 0 0 |

| 4 | Lump sums or benefits received from an Employer Financed Retirement Benefits Scheme excluding pensions |
| £ _____ . 0 0 |

| 5 | Redundancy and other lump sums and compensation payments |
| £ _____ . 0 0 |

| 6 | Tax taken off boxes 3 to 5 |
| £ _____ . 0 0 |

| 7 | If you have left box 6 blank because the tax is included in box 2 on the *Employment* page, put 'X' in the box |
| ☐ |

| 8 | Exemptions for amounts entered in box 4 |
| £ _____ . 0 0 |

| 9 | Compensation and lump sum £30,000 exemption - *see page Ain 24 of the notes* |
| £ _____ . 0 0 |

| 10 | Disability and foreign service deduction |
| £ _____ . 0 0 |

| 11 | Seafarers' Earnings Deduction - *the total amount (and give the names of the ships in the 'Additional information' box on page Ai 4)* |
| £ _____ . 0 0 |

| 12 | Foreign earnings not taxable in the UK |
| £ _____ . 0 0 |

| 13 | Foreign tax for which tax credit relief not claimed |
| £ _____ . 0 0 |

| 14 | Exempt employers' contributions to an overseas pension scheme |
| £ _____ . 0 0 |

These boxes only cover any liability to income tax; if you have made capital gains or losses on disposing of your holdings you may need to declare them in the *Capital gains* supplementary pages (SA108).

## Taxable lump sums, compensation for loss of office and redundancy

**Boxes 3 to 9.** In negotiating termination or compensation of any kind with your employer, the question of what is and is not going to be liable to tax should be discussed in full preferably with independent advisers. Enter the details here.

On page 73, there is general advice and tax tips covering these matters.

## Seafarers' earnings deduction

**Boxes 11 and 17.** A deduction from earnings (a foreign earnings deduction) is available to seafarers working on a ship who have an eligible period of absence from the UK. Fill in the amount (which your employer should provide) in box 11 and the names of the ships in box 17 (see page 64).

## Foreign earnings not taxable in the UK

Most matters relating to overseas earnings are covered in the *Non-residence* supplementary pages (see page 56) and the *Foreign* supplementary pages (see page 47) but surprisingly there are elements of earnings that need to be recorded here.

The whole issue of residence and domicile is very complicated and outside the scope of this book. You are advised to seek professional help to ensure you do not pay more tax than you should. There are copious notes issued by HMRC (help sheet 211) which you can get by telephoning 0845 9000 444.

**Exempt employers' contributions to an overseas pension scheme**
**Box 14.** This enables you to state the amount if you think your employer has made any such contributions. The company should provide you with a statement to this effect at the end of the tax year.

## Other tax reliefs

| | |
|---|---|
| 1 Subscriptions for Venture Capital Trust shares - *the amount on which relief is claimed* | 6 Post-cessation expenses and certain other losses |
| £ ⬚⬚⬚⬚⬚⬚⬚ · 0 0 | £ ⬚⬚⬚⬚⬚⬚⬚⬚ · 0 0 |
| 2 Subscriptions for shares under the Enterprise Investment Scheme - *the amount on which relief is claimed (and provide more information on page Ai 4)* | 7 Maintenance payments (max £2,440) - *only if you or your former spouse or civil partner were born before 6 April 1935* |
| £ ⬚⬚⬚⬚⬚⬚⬚ · 0 0 | £ ⬚⬚⬚⬚ · 0 0 |
| 3 Community Investment Tax Relief - *the amount on which relief is claimed* | 8 Payments to a trade union etc. for death benefits - *half the amount paid (max £100)* |
| £ ⬚⬚⬚⬚⬚⬚⬚ · 0 0 | £ ⬚⬚⬚ · 0 0 |
| 4 Annuities and annual payments made | 9 Relief claimed for employer's compulsory widow's, widower's or orphan's benefit scheme - *(max £22)* |
| £ ⬚⬚⬚⬚⬚⬚⬚ · 0 0 | £ ⬚⬚ · 0 0 |
| 5 Qualifying loan interest payable in the year | 10 Relief claimed on a qualifying distribution on the redemption of bonus shares or securities |
| £ ⬚⬚⬚⬚⬚⬚⬚ · 0 0 | £ ⬚⬚⬚⬚⬚⬚⬚ · 0 0 |

**Boxes 1 and 2.** Information about venture capital trusts and enterprise investment schemes can be found on page 163 of this book, as well as community investment tax relief.

**Box 4.** See page 91.

**Box 5.** Qualifying interest is dealt with on pages 87–88.

**Box 6.** Any income you have *received* after your business ceased trading is dealt with on page 128; conversely you may have had to make later *payments* which are allowed for tax and it is in box 6 that you can claim these.

**Box 7.** See page 88.

**Boxes 8 and 9.** See page 91.

**Box 10.** If you are a higher rate tax payer and have redeemed bonus shares then such payment will have included a tax credit but the receipt of such distribution will have already been declared by you in the dividends box (box 3) on page TR3 of the main tax return. If you do not fill in box 10, then you will be taxed twice on the distribution.

## Age-related married couple's allowance

If you, or your spouse or civil partner, were born **before** 6 April 1935, complete the relevant boxes

**1** Your spouse's or civil partner's full name

**2** Their date of birth if older than you (and at least one of you was born before 6 April 1935) *DD MM YYYY*

**3** If you have already agreed that half the minimum allowance is to go to your spouse or civil partner, put 'X' in the box

**4** If you have already agreed that all of the minimum allowance is to go to your spouse or civil partner, put 'X' in the box

**5** If, in the year to 5 April 2008, you lived with any previous spouse or civil partner, enter their date of birth

**6** If half of the minimum allowance is to be given to you, put 'X' in the box

**7** If all of the minimum allowance is to be given to you, put 'X' in the box

**8** Your spouse's or civil partner's full name

**9** If you were married or formed a civil partnership after 5 April 2007, enter the date of marriage or civil partnership

**10** If you want to have your spouse's or civil partner's surplus allowance, put 'X' in the box

**11** If you want your spouse or civil partner to have your surplus allowance, put 'X' in the box

**Boxes 1 to 11.** Here you can claim the married couple's allowance if either you, your husband or wife or civil partner were born before 6 April 1935; see page 92 for further details and the opportunities for transferring all or part of this allowance to your partner if it will save you tax. Provided one of the partners was born before 6 April 1935 and you married or formed a civil partnership during the 2007–2008 tax year, you can claim a proportion of the annual allowance pro-rata.

## Other information

### Income tax losses

**1** Earlier years' losses - *which can be set against certain other income in 2007-08*

£ · 0 0

**2** Total unused losses carried forward

£ · 0 0

**3** Relief now for 2008-09 trading, or certain capital, losses

£ · 0 0

**4** and tax year for which you are claiming relief in box 3 *YYYY YY*

See page 128 regarding losses and the figures to go in this section of the tax return.

## Pension savings tax charges and taxable lump sums from overseas pension schemes

| 5 | Value of pension benefits in excess of your Available Lifetime Allowance, taken by you as a lump sum | 10 | Amount of unauthorised payment from a pension scheme, subject to Surcharge |
|---|---|---|---|
| £ · 0 0 | | £ · 0 0 | |
| 6 | Value of pension benefits in excess of your Available Lifetime Allowance, not taken as a lump sum | 11 | Foreign tax paid on an unauthorised payment (in £ sterling) |
| £ · 0 0 | | £ · 0 0 | |
| 7 | Lifetime Allowance tax paid by your pension scheme | 12 | Taxable short service refund of contributions (overseas pension schemes only) |
| £ · 0 0 | | £ · 0 0 | |
| 8 | Amount saved towards your pension, in the period covered by this Tax Return, in excess of the Annual Allowance | 13 | Taxable lump sum death benefit payment (overseas pension schemes only) |
| £ · 0 0 | | £ · 0 0 | |
| 9 | Amount of unauthorised payment from a pension scheme, not subject to Surcharge | 14 | Foreign tax paid (in £ sterling) on boxes 12 and 13 |
| £ · 0 0 | | £ · 0 0 | |

Pages 164–167 of this book deal with pension contributions and elements of the new pension legislation that can give rise to tax charges. It is unlikely that this section of the tax return will apply unless you have a high value pension fund or one to which you are making very large annual contributions.

### Tax avoidance schemes

| 15 | The scheme reference number | 16 | The tax year in which the expected advantage arises - year ended 5 April YYYY |
|---|---|---|---|

**Boxes 15 and 16.** These enable you to declare details of any tax avoidance schemes in which you have been involved. You should consult a qualified adviser as to the information required.

### Additional information

| 17 | Please give any additional information in this space |
|---|---|

**Box 17.** You can use this box to give more details about items already declared in these sheets if it will add clarity to the tax office understanding the figures.

# CHAPTER 5

## Your 2008 tax return

# Employment income and benefits, and pensions

This chapter deals with income from employment including any benefits or expense allowances, and redundancy or leaving compensation you have received. Any pensions and social security benefits received are also covered here.

Your earnings and benefits from employment and pension income have to be declared in the *Employment* supplementary pages.

### Wages, salaries, fees, bonuses, etc.

You should have received from your employer a form P60 which shows your earnings for the year and tax deducted under PAYE. You are entitled by law to receive this form by 31 May so do chase your employer if it is not to hand.

Also include in the *Employment* pages of the tax return any salary you received from your husband or wife or civil partner if you were employed in his or her business. You must show your gross earnings before any deductions of income tax and national insurance, but you are allowed to deduct any contributions you make to your employer's pension scheme provided that it is one approved by the tax inspector, or any payroll giving donations.

If your P60 form includes an amount for jobseeker's allowance then, confusingly, this should be shown in box 14 in the Income section of your main tax return. The P60 form may also show earnings from a previous employer, in which case show your current earnings in the boxes on page E1 of the *Employment* pages and previous earnings in the boxes on page E2.

Directors' remuneration is frequently voted on an annual basis. The amount to show in your tax return is usually the amount actually received in the tax year (normally the figure on your P60 form); however, you are taxable on earnings shown in the company's accounts if such sums were available (even if not actually drawn by you) in the tax year.

In addition to your regular PAYE employment, you may have other earnings. These might include casual work, fees and commissions, etc. Providing these incomes are not paid at regular intervals nor paid by the same person, then it is unlikely they will be classed as employment income and so do not enter such income in the *Employment* pages but under the Income section of the main tax return (box 15) – see page 26 of this book. Make sure you claim any relevant expenses in box 16.

Tips and gratuities, if not included in your P60 form, should be shown in box 3 in the *Employment* pages.

## Benefits

### Company cars

Virtually all employees whose earnings and reimbursed expenses, including potential benefits in kind, are at the rate of £8,500 a year or more, and all directors whatever their earnings and expenses, are liable to pay tax on any benefit they have from the use of a company car, and additionally on any fuel used on private journeys if paid for by their employer. These benefits will still be taxable if the car is used by a member of the employee's family or household. Company car and fuel benefits should appear in your coding notice or tax assessment and need to be checked against the information provided by your employer.

The car benefit tax applies to all company cars, including those that are leased, and will be assumed by your tax office to cover all the running costs, even if these amount to more than the tax benefit charge. The cost of a chauffeur, however, will be taxed as a separate benefit.

A taxable benefit will not usually arise if a company car is part of a 'pool', provided that the vehicle is actually used by two or more employees, with any private use being merely incidental, and the vehicle is not normally kept overnight at or near the employee's place of residence.

If a company car is not available for a period of at least 30 consecutive days (for example, if it is in for repair), then the car benefit is reduced proportionately.

### Company car benefit

The tax charge on a company car benefit is calculated as a percentage of the list price of the car, but this percentage is graduated according to carbon dioxide ($CO_2$) emissions.

## Cars with approved $CO_2$ emissions rating

| $CO_2$ emissions in grammes per kilometre (Round down to the nearest multiple) | | | | Taxable benefit |
|---|---|---|---|---|
| 2005–2006 | 2006–2007 | 2007–2008 | 2008–2009 | per cent |
| | | | 120 or less | 10* |
| | | | 135 | 15* |
| 140 | 140 | 140 | 140 | 15* |
| 145 | 140 | 140 | 140 | 16* |
| 150 | 140 | 140 | 140 | 17* |
| 155 | 155 | 155 | 155 | 18* |
| 160 | 160 | 160 | 160 | 19* |
| 165 | 165 | 165 | 165 | 20* |
| 170 | 170 | 170 | 170 | 21* |
| 175 | 175 | 175 | 175 | 22* |
| 180 | 180 | 180 | 180 | 23* |
| 185 | 185 | 185 | 185 | 24* |
| 190 | 190 | 190 | 190 | 25* |
| 195 | 195 | 195 | 195 | 26* |
| 200 | 200 | 200 | 200 | 27* |
| 205 | 205 | 205 | 205 | 28* |
| 210 | 210 | 210 | 210 | 29* |
| 215 | 215 | 215 | 215 | 30* |
| 220 | 220 | 220 | 220 | 31* |
| 225 | 225 | 225 | 225 | 32* |
| 230 | 230 | 230 | 230 | 33** |
| 235 | 235 | 235 | 235 | 34*** |
| 240 | 240 | 240 | 240 | 35**** |

*Notes*
**Diesel supplements if car runs solely on diesel** (waived for cars registered up to 1 January 2006 if Euro IV diesels): *  Add 3 per cent; **add 2 per cent; ***add 1 per cent; **** maximum charge so no diesel supplement.
There is a 2 per cent supplement for cars on E85 fuel from 6 April 2008.

## Taxable benefit for pre-1998 cars and those with no approved $CO_2$ emissions rating

| Engine size (cc) | Pre-1998 car | 1998 or later car | |
|---|---|---|---|
| | | Petrol | Diesel |
| | per cent | per cent | per cent |
| 0–1,400 | 15 | 15 | 18 |
| 1,401–2,000 | 22 | 25 | 28 |
| 2,001 and over† | 32 | 35 | 35 |

*Note* † Also including rotary engined petrol cars which have no cylinder capacity.

There is no reduction for business mileage or the age of the car.

The value of the vehicle for tax purposes is the manufacturer's list price at the time of first registration (less any personal contribution up to £5,000) and including delivery charges, VAT and any accessories over £100 added to the vehicle, unless they were for disabled persons.

There are exceptions for classic cars; the open market value is taken instead of the list price where the car is aged 15 years or more at the end of the tax year and has a market value of £15,000 or more. (There is a cap of £80,000 on the list, or market, price.)

The minimum normal charge will be 10 per cent of the list price for cars with the lowest $CO_2$ emissions with a maximum of 35 per cent for cars with high emissions. Cars without an approved emissions figure (that is all cars registered before 1 January 1998) will be taxed according to engine size (see table on page 67). Discounts are available for cars that run on alternative fuels and technologies. Ask the tax office for leaflet IR172 if you require more information.

Your car's emission figure will either be in the vehicle registration document or available from the manufacturer or dealer, or enquire free of charge on the internet at **www.smmt.co.uk**, or if the car was registered after May 2001, **www.vcacarfueldata.org.uk**.

All the figures in the above charts are reduced by 6 per cent for cars run on electricity, 3 per cent for those run on hybrid electricity and petrol and 2 per cent for those run on gas or bi-fuel gas/petrol.

If your employer pays your congestion charges in London (or elsewhere) they are not regarded as a separate taxable benefit as they are considered to be covered in the taxable benefit you pay on the vehicle.

**Company car private fuel benefit**

If your employer pays for fuel used on your private journeys (and this includes travel from home to your normal business address), then you are taxed on this benefit regardless of your annual business mileage.

A standard figure of £14,400 has been used up until 2007–2008 and the tax benefit is based on the $CO_2$ rating percentage of your vehicle (see table on page 67). **However, for 2008–2009 this base figure is increasing to £16,900.**

For example, if you had a vehicle that used petrol with $CO_2$ emissions of 190 for 2007–2008, then the taxable benefit will be 25 per cent × £14,400 = £3,600.

The tax charge is the maximum that can be levied, even if in practice the cost of private mileage is more.

Is there any way you can avoid the fuel tax charge? Yes – you can pay for all your own private fuel (or reimburse your employer for all the private usage) but if you do this you will have to keep a detailed record each year of every car journey undertaken, both private and business. Bear in mind that travel from your home to your normal place of business is considered to be private mileage for tax purposes.

You may well find it to your advantage to accept the tax charge – it might be less than you would actually pay for private mileage!

## Mileage allowances

If you use your own car on your employer's business you can claim 40p per mile for the first 10,000 business miles in a tax year, and 25p a mile thereafter; this is called 'approved mileage allowance payment' (AMAP); any payment over these figures will be subject to tax and national insurance.

If your employer reimburses less than the mileage figure above, you can claim the difference in your tax return. An extra 5p per mile can be paid by your employer if you have a business passenger, but you cannot claim relief for this if your employer doesn't pay it.

There is no longer an option to claim deductions based on actual expenditure – AMAP has replaced that. You will only need to declare in your tax return the mileage payments you receive if they are in excess of these approved figures.

The motorcycle rates are 24p per business mile and 20p for bicycles for 2007–2008 and 2008–2009.

If you use a company car and you provide the fuel for business travel, you can claim reimbursement from your employer at the following maximum rates per mile (effective from 1 January 2008) without incurring any taxable benefit.

|  | *Petrol* | *Diesel* | *LPG* |
|---|---|---|---|
| 1400cc or less | 11p | 11p | 7p |
| 1400cc to 2000cc | 13p | 11p | 8p |
| Over 2000cc | 19p | 14p | 11p |

## Company vans

Employees benefiting from the private use of a company van pay income tax on a standard 'benefit' of £3,000 a year irrespective of the age of the van. It was confirmed in the budget that this 2007–2008 rate will also apply for 2008–2009. The benefit is apportioned in the case of shared vans.

If you use the van for unrestricted private use, you also pay tax on a fuel benefit of £500 a year but there is no charge where fuel is provided only for home to work journeys.

## Bicycles

Under this scheme your employer can get you a cut price bicycle if you cycle to work.

Most cycle retailers take part in this scheme; your employer pays for the bike (and accessories) – (there is no limit so you can get an expensive one if your employer agrees!) – and leases it back to you over say a 12-month period for an agreed nominal amount. The amount you pay is deducted from your gross salary before tax and national insurance (so this reduces these tax charges); at the end of the lease period, the employer 'sells' the bike to you for a pre-agreed nominal amount on which you will not pay tax. You can't claim the 20p a mile (see above) whilst you lease but you can once you own the bike.

Bear in mind this salary sacrifice, as it is called, could affect either your earnings figure if you are borrowing for a mortgage or your pension entitlement, but the figures should not be significant.

## Living accommodation

Unless there are exceptional circumstances, living accommodation provided by an employer is taxable as a benefit.

The amount assessed will normally equate to the gross rateable value of the property, but if the cost of the property is higher than £75,000 then an additional amount is taxable, based on the market value of the property, less £75,000, multiplied by the official rate of interest which is announced, and varied, by HMRC periodically. Any rent or contribution to upkeep you made to your employer is deductible from the benefit before calculating tax due. You will, however, be assessed on any expenditure paid on your behalf (for example, heating, council tax, etc.).

## Low-interest loan

An employee who has the benefit of a cheap or interest-free loan is taxable on the benefit as compared with the official rate of interest (available from your tax office). Your employer does not need to report loans if the whole of the interest would have been liable for tax relief.

If the total of non-eligible loans does not exceed £5,000 at any time in the tax year or if the loan is made on commercial terms and your employer supplies goods or services on credit to the general public, then no charge is made.

## Other benefits

All employees whose earnings, expenses and potential benefits are at the rate of £8,500 a year or more, and most directors regardless of their earnings or expenses, will probably have had any benefits or perks they have received reported to the tax inspector by their employer. The employer has to do this by law by sending in a form P11D, of which you are entitled to receive a copy by 6 July. However, it is still your responsibility to declare such a perk in your tax return. There are certain benefits or perks that an employer can provide which are tax free. You need not mention them on your tax return if they are not taxable, but see page 80 for dispensations, etc.

Some of the more usual benefits, with a summary of the tax situation, are detailed below.

| **Benefits** | | |
|---|---|---|
| *Benefit* | *Employees earning £8,500 a year or more and directors* | *Employees earning less than £8,500 a year* |
| Armed forces operational allowance | Not taxable | |
| Assets provided for your use free of charge (e.g. video) | Taxable at 20 per cent of initial market value | Usually tax free |
| Bicycles | See page 70 | |
| Canteen facilities | Not taxable if available to all staff | |
| Car and bike parking at work | Not taxable | |
| Cash vouchers | Taxable | |
| Child care costs and vouchers (see page 152) | Not taxable up to £50 per week | |
| Clothing and other goods given by your employer | Taxable | Taxed on secondhand value |
| Company cars, vans, etc. | Taxable | Not taxable |
| Computer equipment | Not taxable on first £2,500 of value | |
| Credit cards (for personal, not business expenditure) | Taxable | |
| Exam prizes | Not taxable if reasonable and not part of employment contract | |

| Benefit | Employees earning £8,500 a year or more and directors | Employees earning less than £8,500 a year |
|---|---|---|
| Fuel for private use of car | Taxable | Not taxable |
| Holidays | Taxable | If employer pays directly, tax-free |
| Interest-free loan | Normally taxable | Not taxable |
| In-house benefits | Taxable on value of the marginal or additional cost to the employer | |
| Living accommodation | Normally taxable unless essential for your employment | |
| Loan of computers/bicycles | Not taxable if less than £2,500 | |
| Luncheon vouchers | Tax free up to 15p per working day | |
| Mileage allowances | Tax free up to the authorised rates – any excess is taxable | |
| Mobile telephones | Not taxable if employer provides | |
| Nurseries and play schemes run by employer | Not taxable if on employer's premises or, if elsewhere, financed by employer | |
| Outplacement counselling | Not taxable | |
| Pension contributions and death-in-service cover | Normally tax-free | |
| Private health schemes | Taxable | Not taxable if company scheme |
| Prizes/incentive awards | Taxable | Not taxable |
| Relocation expenses | Tax-free up to £8,000 (if qualifying) | |
| Retraining and counselling on leaving employment | Not taxable if you have been employed for at least two years | |
| Scholarships provided by employers' trust | Taxable | |
| Season tickets for travel paid directly by employer | Taxable | |
| Share incentive schemes | Not taxable if approved by HMRC | |
| Sick pay schemes | Taxable | |
| Travel to work by bus (free or discounted) | Not taxable in qualifying circumstances | |
| Workplace sports facilities | Not taxable | |

## Leaving payments and compensation

Compensation for loss of office, payment in lieu of notice, ex-gratia payments, redundancy pay and retirement and death lump sums all come under this heading in the tax return. The relevant sections of the tax return are shown on page 61.

The first £30,000 of compensation is tax free, but any excess is taxable. This £30,000 limit has not been increased since 1988!

Note, however, that if your contract of employment gives you a right to compensation on ceasing to be employed, then the lump sum you receive will be taxable, regardless of the amount.

When considering agreements for compensation, it is wise to consult a tax adviser or solicitor to negotiate the terms and the timing, which can be critical, especially on termination of a contract. Any benefits arising after termination will be taxed only when they are actually received or 'enjoyed', rather than being taken into account in the actual redundancy year.

An example is given overleaf of the various tax calculations that have to be considered when assessing the impact of redundancy pay. In the example shown, when John sends in his 2008 self assessment tax return he will include the redundancy payment and will pay any tax due to the tax office by 31 January 2009.

When submitting your tax return, make sure you fill in the relevant boxes on page Ai2 of the *Additional information* supplementary pages (SA101 – see page 61 in this book).

## An example of the tax calculations arising on the receipt of redundancy pay

John was made redundant during the 2007–2008 tax year. His total earnings for the year were £40,000 and he was awarded a redundancy payment of £90,000.

|  |  |  | £ |
|---|---|---|---|
| Earnings |  |  | 40,000.00 |
| Less: Personal allowance, say |  |  | 5,225.00 |
|  |  |  | 34,775.00 |
| Tax liability | £ 2,230 at 10 per cent |  | 223.00 |
|  | £32,370 at 22 per cent |  | 7,121.40 |
|  | £ 175 at 40 per cent |  | 70.00 |
|  | £33,565 | Tax due | 7,414.40 |

A redundancy payment of £90,000 is to be made after the form P45 has been issued. The employer will deduct tax as follows:

|  | £ |
|---|---|
| Redundancy | 90,000 |
| Less: Tax-free limit | 30,000 |
|  | 60,000 |
| Less: Tax on £60,000 at 22 per cent | 13,200 |
|  | £46,800 |

Once the employer has notified the tax office of this redundancy payment, they will then review the tax position as follows:

|  | £ |
|---|---|
| Earnings | 40,000 |
| Add: Redundancy after tax-free limit | 60,000 |
|  | 100,000 |
| Less: Personal allowance | 5,225 |
|  | 94,775 |

| Tax liability calculated as: |  | £ |
|---|---|---|
| £ 2,230 at 10 per cent |  | 223.00 |
| £32,370 at 22 per cent |  | 7,121.40 |
| £60,175 at 40 per cent |  | 24,070.00 |
| £94,775 | £ | 31,414.40 |
| Less: Tax already collected (as above) | 7,414.40 |  |
| Deducted from redundancy payment | 13,200.00 | 20,614.40 |
| Additional tax due |  | £10,800.00 |

## Expense allowances

Round-sum allowances are taxable as income unless an employee (and such term includes a director) can identify accurately the expenditure involved and satisfy the tax office that such sums were spent wholly, exclusively and necessarily on the employer's business.

Refer also to Chapter 6 (see page 78).

## Share schemes

There are many approved share schemes that now offer tax incentives to encourage employees' involvement in companies, but the rules are complicated and vary from scheme to scheme. The relevant sections of the tax return are reproduced on page 60. Some schemes are unapproved and do not qualify for the same level of tax benefits.

The following gives a very brief summary of the main types of scheme and the tax benefits associated with them.

### Savings-related share schemes (save as you earn)

Employees pay a monthly sum via their employer into a savings-related share option scheme over a predetermined period at the end of which, the savings, plus a tax-free bonus, are used to purchase shares at a fixed price. (There is a minimum of £5 a month and a maximum of £250 a month.) This price must not be less than 80 per cent of the market value at the time of the option. No income tax or national insurance is payable on the option grant or on exercising the option.

No capital gain arises if shares up to a value of £7,200 (£7,000 for 2007–2008) are transferred into an ISA within certain time limits.

### Approved share incentive plans

Employees are able to allocate part of their salary to acquire partnership shares in the company that employs them, without paying tax or national insurance, from which the employer is also exempt. Additionally, an employer can award free shares for participating employees and/or you can allocate your dividends to buy more shares.

There are maximum limits depending on the type of shares and various periods of ownership (usually five years) required to benefit fully from the tax advantages.

### Company share option schemes

An employer grants to an employee an option to purchase shares at a fixed price (which must not be discounted) at a future date. No income tax or national insurance is payable on the granting of the option nor on any proceeds of sale, provided you take up the option between three and ten years.

## Approved profit-sharing schemes

New schemes have not been possible since 31 December 2002 but you may still be holding such free shares, which will be held by a trust on your behalf. They are tax free if held for at least three years.

## Enterprise management incentives

Employers can offer these incentive share options to their staff. They are free of income tax and both employer's and employee's national insurance. If the shares were sold before 5 April 2008, capital gains taper relief will date from the time that the option was granted, rather than the date it was exercised, but note that taper relief is being abolished from that date (see Chapter 15, on page 134).

There are tax rules and regulations that identify the type of company that can grant these incentives and a definition of employees that are eligible to receive them.

## Foreign income

There are *Foreign* supplementary pages to the tax return which specifically deal with people who normally live in the UK but have savings, property income or benefits from overseas (see page 47).

There are measures intended to protect employees from paying tax twice on the same income, principally the double taxation agreements held with various countries throughout the world, and these are detailed in the notes that come with these supplementary pages.

Special concessions exist for seafarers (see page 61).

If you receive a pension as a result of employment with an overseas Government, only 90 per cent of the pension is taxable (see box 10 in your main tax return).

Before you take up an appointment abroad, check carefully, both with your employer and with your tax office, as to how foreign earnings in your particular instance will be treated for tax purposes.

You will be classed as a non-resident for tax purposes if you live and work abroad for at least the whole of a tax year provided your visits back to the UK do not, on average, amount to more than 91 days in a tax year. This means that your earnings from overseas will be tax free.

If you are a UK resident, any foreign earnings will be taxable in the UK.

Keep an eye on the national insurance situation – you don't want to lose your rights to UK State benefits because you have not paid enough NI contributions. Ask for HMRC leaflet N138 and DWP leaflet SA 29 which clarifies this complicated area.

## Income from pensions

All your pension income, including the State retirement pension, has to be declared on page TR3 of your main tax return. Refer to page 25 of this book for advice on how to fill in the various boxes. If you have pension income from private pension schemes in addition to the State pension then it is important that you check at the end of the tax year how much tax has been deducted to see if you are due a refund. See Chapter 12, on page 108, on how to go about this.

Due to the major restructuring in the pension legislation that took place in April 2006, there may be tax liabilities if you have exceeded certain limits in terms of the value of your pension fund, or amounts of your annual pension contributions, or indeed if your pension scheme was unapproved by HMRC. There is a new section this year in the *Additional information* pages to declare any potential liability (see page 64). Refer to page 166 in this book for advice.

## State benefits received

It is under the *Income* section, on page TR3 of your main tax return, that you need to declare any State benefits received. The tax treatment of these benefits is extremely complicated and it would take a separate book to cover all the legislation.

However, as an overview, you need to declare in box 12 of your main tax return any taxable incapacity benefit (excepting the first 28 weeks) and declare the total of all the following benefits in box 14:

- Bereavement allowance and widow's pension.

- Carer's allowance.

- Industrial death benefit paid as a pension.

- Jobseeker's allowance.

- Statutory sick, maternity, paternity and adoption pay if paid by HMRC (if paid by your employer it would have been included in your P60 earnings declared in your *Employment* pages).

Exclude any amounts included in any of the above that are paid for child dependency or child allowance.

Chapter 2 lists those social security benefits that are exempt from tax and do not have to be declared in your tax return (see page 12).

Use the working sheets at the back of this book to keep a record of the details making up the totals you declare in your tax return in case the tax office require the information at a later date.

# CHAPTER 6

## Your 2008 tax return

# Claiming expenses against your income

There are certain types of expenditure which, if necessary for your job and provided at your expense, may be claimed against your income. Fill in the appropriate boxes in the expenses section of the *Employment* supplementary pages of your tax return. To assist your claim it may be worthwhile obtaining a letter from your employer confirming that whilst your expenses are justified and necessary for your job, they are not reimbursed as a matter of policy.

It is important to keep a record of the details and dates on which the expenditure was incurred, and the receipts where possible. Some allowable expenses are listed below.

### Factory, manual, shop and healthcare workers

Extra costs incurred by employees working temporarily away from home. Lorry drivers and construction site workers have special concessions.

- Overalls, boiler suits, boots, helmets, gloves and other special protective clothing. You should also include the cost of cleaning and repairing such items.

- Tools, toolbags and equipment.

- Travelling expenses (but see page 80).

- Trade journals and technical books essential to your job.

- Trade unions often agree with the tax inspector a fixed allowance which you can claim to cover certain expenses (for example, engineers £45 to £120; agricultural workers £70). Alternatively, keep a record of all your expenses and submit an annual claim.

- Working rule agreements which exist between the tax office and various construction industry representatives and healthcare workers have set guidelines regarding the expenses you can claim.

## Sales representatives, office and clerical workers

- Travelling and hotel expenses on company business.

- If you use your own car for business travel, then you can claim the mileage allowances shown on page 69.

- Technical and other books on your firm's products or services. It may be advisable to obtain a letter from your employer confirming that this expenditure is necessary for your job.

- Telephone – part of your own telephone bill covering calls to customers, etc.

- Gifts to customers paid for by yourself which do not cost more than £50 per customer per year and which advertise your firm's products or services. (The gift must not be food, drink, tobacco or a voucher.)

- Fees or subscriptions paid to an organisation of which you are a member. The organisation must be on the HMRC approved list.

- Journals and publications essential to your employment or profession.

## Seafarer's deduction

A deduction from earnings (a foreign earnings deduction) is available to seafarers working on a ship who have an eligible period of absence from the UK (see page 61).

## Use of your home as an office

If you are required to do work for your employer at home, and use a specific room for this purpose, you ought to claim an allowance based on a proportion of total upkeep, for example, rent, light, heat, insurance, cleaning, repairs to furniture, etc. Such a claim should be made in box 20 'other expenses' on the *Employment* supplementary pages in your tax return. (See also pages 120 and 141 regarding business use and capital gains tax.) Your employer is able to pay a tax and national insurance free allowance of £2 per week to cover the additional costs of working at home. Whilst this is a modest amount, it does not need to be supported by receipts.

## Capital allowances

If you use equipment such as a computer, provided by yourself, which is essential for your work, then you can claim capital allowances. This does not apply if you use your own car whilst on your employer's business – the official mileage allowance (see page 69) is considered to include a sum in lieu of capital allowances.

## Travelling expenses

You are able to claim travelling expenses as a tax deduction against your income if they have not been reimbursed by your employer, provided the journeys were not repetitive, that is from your home to a permanent place of work. This means that if your work takes you to many different locations, even if you start from home each day, then such expenses can be claimed. However, if you routinely visit a different office or branch each day of the week you may have more than one permanent workplace.

The tax legislation is complicated, but where a site-based employee is working for more than 24 months at that workplace, it will be regarded as permanent and travelling expenses from home to site will not be allowed for tax.

## Incidental overnight expenses

Miscellaneous personal expenses up to £5 a night paid by the employer whilst away from home on business in the UK (£10 a night abroad) are tax free.

## Interest payments

If you have to borrow money to buy equipment (such as a computer) necessary for your job, then the interest can be claimed as an expense against your income. Relief for car loans was withdrawn from 6 April 2002. Interest on a bank overdraft or credit card is not allowable.

## Employees earning £8,500 or more, and directors

As explained on page 71, your employer has to send to the tax office a form P11D, which details expenses and benefits that you have received. There is a legal obligation for all employers to give their employees copies of these forms by 6 July, which will be a help in checking your tax.

Refer to Chapter 5 (page 65), which covers all such benefits.

You might receive a letter from your tax office asking for details of these expenses, and you must then convince them that you did not receive any personal benefit or, if you did, obtain their agreement on the proportion of the expenses to be disallowed. You will pay tax on this proportion.

Sometimes an employer can arrange with the tax office to get a dispensation making it unnecessary to complete certain parts of form

P11D, in which case the employee does not need to include such expenses in their tax return.

The major conditions for a dispensation are normally that the reimbursement of expenses is closely supervised and it is obvious that the expenses themselves are easily justifiable (for example, travelling and subsistence expenses for a representative).

Even if a dispensation is granted, the expenses still have to be taken into account in deciding if an employee's total remuneration, including reimbursed expenses, is £8,500 or more.

An employer may also make an arrangement to meet the tax liability on behalf of employees in respect of certain benefits. This is known as a PAYE settlement agreement and may cover items such as Christmas gifts, awards and shared benefits.

# CHAPTER 7

## Your 2008 tax return

# Income from savings, investments, property and trusts, etc.

This chapter deals with income from land and property, dividends and interest from investments and trusts and also maintenance which you may need to declare in your tax return. This section of the tax return is shown on pages 24–25 of this book.

### Assets held in joint names

If a husband and wife or civil partner have income from an asset held in joint names, it is assumed to be divided equally when filling in your respective tax returns. If the ownership is not held equally, then you should ask the tax office for form 17 on which you can jointly declare the actual ownership split. You then enter the amounts accordingly in your tax returns. Such declaration takes effect from the date it is made, provided the form is sent to the tax office within 60 days.

Prior to 6 April 2004, any distributions on shares in close companies owned jointly by a husband and wife have automatically been split 50:50 for tax purposes unless an election has been made as above. However, since that date, distributions such as dividends have been taxed according to the actual proportions of ownership and entitlement to the income without the need for an election.

### Interest from savings and investments

This interest has to be declared in your tax return in boxes 1 to 6. This section of the return is reproduced on page 24 of this book. You will need to differentiate between interest that has had tax deducted and that which has been paid gross. Use the working sheets at the back of this book as you only have to show the totals, not the detail, in your tax return.

If you have joint savings or investments, only include your share of the income in your tax return. Refer to page 150 as to whether you can save tax by changing some of your investments to joint holdings.

Show all your income from National Savings and investments in this section but exclude the first £70 of interest earned on any ordinary account that you may still have.

You do not have to include interest from National Savings certificates as that is tax free.

Investment account interest with National Savings is credited automatically to your account on 31 December – you can request a statement and the tax office will accept this figure to go in your return. You do not have to apportion it on a time basis.

Remember to include National Savings interest from income or capital bonds under this section of the return. The interest is taxed on an annual basis even though it is not actually received until the bond is repaid after five years. Include also details of first option bonds and fixed rate savings bonds.

There is no need to enter interest from SAYE account as it is not taxable, nor is interest from PEPs, ISAs etc.

For a general review of savings and the tax implications see Chapter 18 (page 157).

If your total income is below your personal allowances then your bank or building society does not have to deduct tax from the interest before you receive it. See page 155 as to the action you should take.

### Dividends from shares in UK companies

Enter in your tax return the amounts that you actually received as shown on your dividend slips. The date on the dividend slip is considered as being the date receivable for tax return purposes. Show income from most unit trusts here, including the income that was reinvested in further units instead of being paid direct to you. The treatment of these tax credits is shown on page 103.

Scrip dividends should also be included here – the dividend statement should show 'the appropriate amount in cash', which is the dividend.

Do not include any equalisation receipts.

### Purchased life annuities

These are covered in the Pensioners chapter on page 115.

## Accrued income securities

Where fixed-interest securities are sold or purchased and the contract note includes an adjustment for accrued interest, this will need to be reported on your tax return unless the nominal value of all your accrued income securities does not exceed £5,000 in the tax year concerned.

The rules are complicated, but the notes accompanying your tax return will include further guidance and HMRC are looking at proposals to simplify the scheme in the future.

## Property income

The tax return supplementary pages *UK property* cover all aspects of UK property income (see page 44).

If a husband and wife or civil partner own a property that is let, the tax office will assume that any income from these assets is divided equally. You should enter in your tax return one half of the income and expenses, and tick the relevant box to indicate to the tax office that it is a joint holding. If the ownership is not held equally, then refer above as to the action you should take.

For the purposes of income tax, all income from property in the UK, including furnished, unfurnished and holiday lettings, is taxable on the same 'commercial' basis as any other business (see Chapter 13, page 118) – that is, expenditure is allowable against profits if it is wholly and exclusively for business purposes. Rent-a-room relief continues to be available, however.

To benefit from the furnished holiday letting tax rules, your property must be *available* for letting at a commercial rent for at least 140 days in each tax year, *actually* let for a minimum of 70 days and not rented out for a continuous period of more than 31 days to the same person in any 155 days period (the tax laws are never straightforward!). One of the main advantages of a furnished holiday letting is that you can claim capital allowances on the cost of equipping and furnishing a property.

## Property expenses

If you receive rents from a property which you let furnished or unfurnished you can claim the following expenses, if applicable:

- Rent paid and water rates.

- General maintenance and repairs of the property, garden and furniture and fittings.

- Costs of agents for letting and collecting rents.

- Insurance, including insurance premium tax.

- Interest payable on a loan to purchase, or improve, investment property (but see page 88 for restrictions).

- Charges for preparing inventories.

- Legal fees on renewing a tenancy agreement, for leases of not more than 50 years, or on the initial grant of a lease not exceeding 21 years.

- Accountancy fees to prepare and agree your income.

- Costs of collecting rents, which could in some cases include your travelling expenses to and from the property.

- Costs of services such as porters, cleaners, security.

- Wear and tear allowance for furniture and fittings: generally 10 per cent of the basic rent receivable. As an alternative, the cost of renewals may be claimed.

- Council tax.

- Expenditure of up to £1,500 for the installation of loft insulation and/or cavity wall insulation in residential property between 6 April 2004 and 5 April 2009; this was extended to cover solid wall insulation from 7 April 2005 and draught proofing and insulation of hot water systems from 6 April 2006 (see page 126).

### Rent-a-room relief

Owner-occupiers and tenants who let furnished accommodation in their own or main home are able to receive rent up to £4,250 a year exempt from income tax. Make sure you tell your insurers and your mortgage company if you enter into a rent-a-room arrangement.

If rent exceeds these limits, you have the option of either paying tax on the excess without any deduction for allowable expenses, or calculating any profit made (gross rents less actual allowable expenses) and paying tax on that profit in the normal way.

An individual's exempt limit is halved if, at any time during a tax year, someone else received income from letting in the same property.

## Income from trusts and settlements, etc.

Normally most estates of deceased persons will have a professional executor or administrator. They should provide you with a form R185, which will identify payments made to you, the rate of tax deducted and the type of trust. If you do not receive this form, then seek advice as to the details you need to include in your tax return.

Income from 'bare' trusts are considered as your own income as you effectively have control, and any income should be shown in the main tax return or relevant supplementary pages.

The tax return has supplementary pages covering *Trusts, etc.* (see page 51).

You may be able to claim tax back (see page 155) in respect of income from discretionary trusts if you are not a higher rate taxpayer.

In these supplementary pages you also have to give details of settlements made, for although capital or income may not have been received by you, it may be considered by the tax office to be your income for tax purposes. The most common example would be income from gifts you may have made to minor children. (See also page 153.)

## Children's income

If you have made gifts of capital to your children who are under the age of 18, the total income resulting from the gifts should be included in your tax return as savings income if it is in excess of £100 gross (but see also page 153).

# CHAPTER 8

## Your 2008 tax return

# Tax reliefs you can claim

This chapter covers payments made by you which may be allowed for tax relief and should be shown on your tax return. These could include interest charges on loans, covenants and donations to charities, maintenance payments, payments to tax-efficient investments, post-cessation expenses and payments to trade unions and friendly societies.

The relevant sections of the tax return are reproduced on pages 28 and 62 of this book.

### Interest on loans for the purchase of private residence

This relief was completely withdrawn from April 2000.

### Interest on other loans

There are other types of loans (called 'qualifying loans'), the interest on which is allowed for tax (see page 62).

They include loans to buy shares or lend to:

- A closely controlled trading company where you or a relative own more than 5 per cent of the company's shares or, if less, you have worked for the greater part of your time in the management of the company. Such interest is not allowed for tax if the shares qualified for tax relief under the business expansion scheme or enterprise investment scheme.

- A partnership.

- A co-operative, provided you work for it full time.

- An employee-controlled trading company (share acquisition only).

- Loans to pay inheritance tax or buy plant or machinery for business use also qualify.

- Loans to buy an annuity if the person buying that annuity was aged 65 or over, the loan was secured on the individual's main residence in the UK or Republic of Ireland and the loan was taken out before 9 March 1999 (or other loans have replaced the original loan). Relief for these loans is restricted to the basic rate of tax up to a maximum loan of £30,000. You can request help sheet IR340 for more information about what you can claim. You may also find the tax office helpline useful – telephone 0845 900 0444.

## Interest paid on loans to buy an investment property

Property investments are assessed on the same basis as any other business (see page 120) – that is, the expenditure is allowable against profits if it is wholly and exclusively for business purposes.

Do not enter interest on a loan to buy an investment property in your main tax return; this has to be entered in the *UK property* supplementary pages (refer to page 44).

The interest rules also extend to overseas properties as well as those in the UK.

## Retirement annuity payments and personal pensions

Refer to pages 164–167 for a summary of the tax-efficient opportunities that can arise from pension planning.

## Hire purchase and credit card interest

You cannot claim relief on this type of interest unless you pay it in connection with your business activities.

## Interest on overdue tax

This cannot be claimed as a deduction for tax purposes.

## Maintenance and alimony payments

You can only get tax relief for maintenance and alimony payments if you, or your former husband, wife or civil partner, were born before 6 April 1935 and you make legally enforceable payments. The maximum relief that can be claimed is the lower of the actual maintenance payments made or £2,540 for 2008–2009 (£2,440 for 2007–2008) and relief is only given at 10 per cent. Such relief ceases if your former husband, wife or civil partner has remarried in 2007–2008.

## Venture capital trusts and enterprise investment schemes

It is in the Reliefs section of the *Additional information* pages of your tax return that you need to state details of the investments. See page 163 for the tax advantages.

There is also a facility in this section to claim relief for any subscription to a community development finance institution (CDFI). State the amount you invested. Relief will be at 5 per cent per year of the amount you lend or invest for up to five years, or the amount that reduces your tax bill to zero for that year.

## Giving to charities under gift aid

The opportunities for giving to charities in a tax-efficient way have been considerably widened in the last few years. The sections of the tax return under which you can claim relief for giving to charity are shown on page 28. The five main options are: payroll giving schemes; covenants; cash donations under a gift aid scheme; the gifting of shares, securities, properties, etc. and donating your tax repayment directly to a charity.

### Payroll giving schemes

Employers are allowed to run these schemes under which an employee can make donations to charity.

The donation is deducted from your pay and passed on to the charity by your employer. PAYE is calculated on your salary after making the deduction so that you are effectively getting immediate tax relief on the donation at your highest tax rate.

There is no need to mention this in your tax return as you will have declared your net earnings after the deduction has been made in the *Employment* supplementary pages.

### Covenants to charities

Prior to 6 April 2000, covenants were used to transfer income in a tax-efficient way to charities; to be effective for income tax purposes they needed to be for more than three years.

You deducted tax from a payment under a deed of covenant at the basic rate and were able to get higher rate tax relief if applicable by claiming on your tax return.

Since the extension of the gift aid scheme there is no need for these types of covenant although existing covenants are still valid for tax relief.

### Gifts of cash
This scheme applies to single gifts made by individuals and companies. There is no minimum limit for donations. Gifts are regarded as being made net of basic rate tax and charities are able to claim repayment of the tax. Relief is also available to non-residents who are liable to tax in the UK.

higher rate tax relief can be claimed where applicable by filling in the appropriate boxes in your tax return (see page 28).

Most charities have gift aid declaration forms for you to complete when you make a donation that will enable them to reclaim the tax.

If you do not pay tax, you should not use gift aid, otherwise you will eventually have to reimburse the tax office for the basic rate tax deducted. The tax office publish a free booklet (IR65) on *Giving to charity*.

### Carry-back and carry-forward relief
In the tax return in box 7 you can elect to have any gift aid payments made after 5 April 2007 backdated to the 2006–2007 tax year for tax relief purposes. Similarly, in box 8, you can treat any payments made between 5 April 2008 and the date you file your tax return (31 January 2009 at the latest) backdated to 2007–2008. It is up to you, not the tax office, to decide whether you wish to do this – obviously you would only do so if it saved you tax, as it will do in the vast majority of cases.

### Gifts of shares, securities, land and buildings
You can gift quoted shares and securities to charities and the full market value of the gift as well as the costs of transfer can be offset against your taxable income.

Similarly you can gift land and buildings to charities.

Individuals should enter the amount in boxes 9 or 10 of their tax return. There is no limit to the value of the gift, and in addition to income tax relief, the share sale or transfer to the charity will be free of capital gains tax.

If you are contemplating making a gift of shares or property to a charity and you are already making a profit on them, then it would be more tax efficient if you gave the assets directly to the charity rather than selling them first. It would also benefit the charity more, tax-wise.

## Donating your tax repayment to charity

If you are due a tax repayment then you can nominate that all, or part, of it is paid directly to a charity of your choice. You need to complete the form *Giving your tax repayment to charity* which you will find in your tax return pack. If you don't know the charity number, then telephone the helpline on 0845 9000 444.

## Trade annuities and patent royalties

If you made these payments for genuine commercial reasons in connection with your trade or profession, then box 4 of the *Additional information* pages of your tax return enables you to claim additional relief if you are a higher rate taxpayer as they will have been treated as having been made after basic rate tax has been deducted.

## Payments to trade unions and friendly societies

If you make compulsory payments to provide annuities for widows and orphans where relief is not given by your employer, or if part of your trade union subscription relates to a pension, insurance or funeral benefit, or you have a friendly society policy providing sickness and death benefits, then you can claim tax relief on one half of the payments in box 8 in the *Additional information* pages (see page 62).

# CHAPTER 9

# Personal tax allowances and tax credits

A tax allowance is not a payment; it is the amount of income you can receive without paying tax. Apart from the personal allowance, all allowances are claimed by filling in a tax return.

The allowances for 2008–2009 as announced in the budget are as follows (for allowances for previous years see page 187).

## Personal allowance

From the moment that someone is born, they are entitled to a basic personal tax allowance each year.

| Age as at 6 April 2008 | £ |
|---|---|
| Under 65 | 5,435 |
| Between 65 and 74* | 9,030 |
| 75 and over* | 9,180 |

Notes
*These age-related allowances are, however, restricted if your income is over £21,800. For every £2 of income above this limit, your allowance is reduced by £1, but no taxpayer can get less than the basic personal allowance of £5,435.

## The married couple's allowance

The term 'married couple' also applies to same-sex couples who have registered their relationship in a civil partnership after 5 December 2005; therefore such couples can claim the same tax allowances as a married couple.

The married couple's allowance was abolished from 6 April 2000 except for couples where either the husband or wife was born before 6 April 1935 or where one person born before this date has married on or after 6 April 2000. The allowances for 2008–2009 are £6,535 (age between 65 and 74) and £6,625 for those aged 75 and over.

Relief is restricted to 10 per cent and the allowance is reduced, depending on your income level, by £1 for every £2 that your income exceeds the income limit of £21,800, but it cannot be reduced below the minimum amount of £2,540.

The personal allowance income restriction (see above) is applied before restricting the married couple's allowance.

In a heterosexual marriage, the wife can claim one half of the married couple's allowance, or indeed the whole allowance, if her husband agrees. Ask your tax office for form 18, but this has to be submitted before the start of the tax year to which it relates.

If it is preferred that the husband gets the whole of the married couple's allowance then there is no need to take any action.

In the case of civil partnerships, the allowance will initally go to the partner with the highest income, but again a request can be made to transfer one half, or the whole allowance, between partners.

## Blind person's allowance

A registered blind person is entitled to an extra tax allowance of £1,800 for 2008–2009 (£1,730 for 2007–2008). This is also claimable by blind persons in the year preceding the year in which they were officially registered blind if, at the end of the previous year, evidence was available to support the eventual registration. The allowance is transferable to a husband or wife, or between civil partners, even if he or she is not blind.

## Children's tax credit and working families tax credit

These tax credits started on 6 April 2001 and ceased on 5 April 2003. It proved very difficult to calculate whether you were entitled to these benefits or not and the administration of them was often chaotic. However, if you *were* entitled to either of these credits and forgot to claim them you can *still* do so by claiming arrears – the telephone helpline is 0845 300 3900.

Also many families that did claim at the appropriate time had great problems in getting the correct amounts paid to them on time, sometimes causing financial hardship. If you were involved in additional expenditure because of administrative errors, then the tax office will reimburse you. You could claim for such things as telephone calls, or extra overdraft or loan interest that you incurred. Write to the tax credit office at Preston, PR1 0SB.

These credits were replaced with the child tax credit and working tax credit from 6 April 2003.

## Child tax credit (CTC)

This is a payment that is made by HMRC to help support families with children. It started in April 2003 and is made up of various elements as detailed in Appendix 5 on page 185.

You can claim for each child or young person up to 1 September following their 16th birthday (and up to age 20 if they are in full-time education) if you are responsible for looking after them. You do not have to be in paid employment to claim it. Claiming the child tax credit does not affect your entitlement to child benefit which, like the child tax credit, is not taxable and does not have to be declared on your tax return.

In spite of its name, the child tax credit will be paid directly to the responsible person and not through the tax system.

The chart reproduced in Appendix 5 shows the figures for 2007–2008 and those announced in the budget for 2008–2009.

### Is it means tested?
Yes it is, but you can have joint income up to £58,170 a year (and up to £66,342 a year if you have a child under one year old) before you lose the benefit, so the earnings levels are quite generous. The child tax credit is not taxable.

### What income is considered?
If you are single (or separated), your claim will be based on your income; if you are a married couple, or a man and a woman living together as if you are married, or in a civil partnership, then your combined total income will be taken into account.

Total income is considered to include earnings from employment or self-employment, some social security benefits, income from savings and investments including rents (but excluding rent-a-room income). You are, however, allowed to deduct payments into a pension scheme and donations to gift aid before the credit is calculated; the calculation also ignores the first £300 of any pension income, property or investment income or foreign income.

### If your circumstances change
Your income levels for 2006–2007 will have been used for assessing any 2008 entitlement. If a change occurs in your circumstances – for example, your earnings take you into a higher band, or you have further children, you change jobs or your marital status changes – you must tell the tax office, either by filling in form TC602 or by telephoning the helpline 0845 300 3900 (0845 603 2000 in Northern Ireland). If you do not advise of changed circumstances then you may have to repay any tax credit overpayments.

However, the tax authorities will not ask for repayment of your entitlement if the increase in your annual income between your declared income and actual income for the year is no greater than £25,000 (this figure is the same for 2007–2008 and 2008–2009).

If you are due extra child tax credit it will only be backdated for three months, so keep vigilant.

Once your annual income exceeds the limits for child tax credit or working tax credit (see below), the sequence in which you start to lose credits is: firstly the basic working tax credit is withdrawn, then any childcare element and finally the child element of the child tax credit is lost.

Once the upper earnings limit is reached, you lose the family element of the child tax credit.

## Further information

For further information, telephone the claim line on 0845 300 3900. There is also a do-it-yourself calculator on the tax credits website **www.directgov.uk**, which will give you a better idea of whether it is worth claiming. Remember that if you are eligible for claiming these tax credits you would also be entitled to a larger child trust fund payment (see page 151).

In addition to the child tax credit you may also be eligible for the working tax credit.

## Working tax credit (WTC)

This is a payment to top up the earnings of those who are in low-income employment, including workers who do not have children. The amount you will receive will depend on your income level, the number of hours you work, your age, whether you have any children for whom you are caring and whether you are involved in paying for childcare to a registered provider. The calculation is very complicated but Appendix 5 gives a broad idea of likely benefit levels (see page 185).

Any childcare element is paid directly to the person responsible for paying for that care. If you are self-employed, the WTC claim will be paid to you directly.

The telephone helpline and claim line for more information are the same as for the child tax credit above: 0845 300 3900.

As with the child tax credit, you must keep the tax office informed of any change in circumstances otherwise you will either not get all the tax credit to which you are entitled or you may have to repay sums where you have claimed too much.

The working tax credit is not taxable.

## Overpayment

If the tax authorities have overpaid your working tax credit or child tax credit and it is not your fault, if you can prove that was so, then you do not have to repay any overpayment. Ask for Form TC846 to establish this claim.

## Annual review of tax credits

You will be sent a review form each year and, depending on your circumstances, also an annual declaration form which you must complete and return. Do this promptly as there are strict time limits for each award period and these will be shown on your form.

## Pension credit

The pension credit was introduced in October 2003 and is designed to top up the weekly income of people aged 60 or over to a guaranteed minimum level.

This pension credit, which is means tested and which is administered by the Pension Service (part of the Department for Work and Pensions), is made up of two parts, the guarantee credit and a savings credit.

### The guarantee credit

This replaced the minimum income guarantee and applies to anyone who is 60 or over and whose income is less than £124.05 (£119.05 for 2007–2008) a week for a single person and £189.35 (£181.70 for 2007–2008) for a couple (it is the age of the older partner that counts for this credit). The pension credit will top up your income to these amounts.

If you are a couple, your combined income is taken into account. The term 'couple' not only means a husband and wife, but also encompasses a person with whom you live 'as if you are married to them' (this is the wording in the tax legislation).

Same-sex couples will need to claim as single people once they have entered into a statutory civil registration procedure.

You may get more if you are severely disabled, looking after a person who is severely disabled, or you have commitments to certain housing costs (for example, mortgage interest payments).

### The savings credit

This is only applicable to those aged 65 or over. For a couple, at least one person must have reached the age of 65.

Under this part of the pension credit, you get extra money if you have income from savings where your savings exceed £6,000

(£10,000 if in a care home). Savings (or capital as the legislation calls it) excludes the value of your own house, personal possessions and life policy surrender values but does include tax-exempt savings accounts (such as ISAs).

The fact that you may be living with your grown-up family does not mean that you cannot claim the pension credit – the claim is based on your income only; also, the fact that you own your own house does not mean that you cannot apply for the credit.

### How to claim

You do not have to fill in complicated forms, which is just as well because to do the calculations yourself would need another book of explanations, for the formulae used for both parts of the pension credit calculation are unbelievably complicated.

To claim, telephone the Pension Service on 0800 99 1234 (0808 601 8821 in Northern Ireland). The text phone number is 0800 1690 133.

They will fill in the form for you and send the completed form to you for signature. You will need to tell them your national insurance number, your bank and savings details, and the amounts of any other pension you receive in addition to the State pension. They will also ask you for details of your housing costs. You will need to tell them into which account you would like your pension credit paid.

You can request a blank application form to fill in yourself if you don't want to get involved in a long telephone conversation, or you can download it from **www.thepensionservice.gov.uk/pensioncredit**.

If you have forgotten to claim, then you can get your application backdated for up to three months. The pension credit is not taxable.

The credit is paid weekly in advance directly into your bank, building society or post office account. If you have difficulty due to a mental or physical disability, it can be paid to you by cheque.

### Re-assessment

You don't have to go through this claims procedure every year. Once your income is assessed at retirement, it is normally re-assessed every five years but you should notify the Pensions Service if your circumstances change materially, for example, getting married, moving house, or you have a significant change in earnings compared with when you first registered or you started to receive social security benefits.

If you disagree with any decision concerning your pension credit, then you should ask for it to be reviewed, but don't delay for too long for most re-assessments have very strict time limits – often within one month of the original notification.

# CHAPTER 10

# PAYE and tax codes

The Pay As You Earn system was introduced to enable every employee to pay tax by instalments rather than in one hefty amount at the end of the tax year. By law, your employer has to deduct PAYE tax and national insurance from your earnings.

## How does an employer know how much to deduct?

You are allocated a tax code by your tax office, and that tells your employer how much you can earn before you start to pay tax. The code is a shortened method of defining your total tax-free pay (usually the total of your allowances), but in fact the last figure is omitted. The code effectively spreads your allowances evenly throughout the tax year. For example, a code 543L means that you start paying tax after you have earned £5,435 (£104.52 each week).

A PAYE coding notice is sent to you if your code changes; it details your allowances, benefits, untaxed income, etc., and shows your tax code. If you do not receive one, you can request a copy from your tax office. You will need to quote your tax reference and national insurance number.

Your employer is also advised of the new tax code but he is not given the details as to how it is compiled so he cannot check it for you.

You should make sure that all allowances due to you are included and be sure your code is amended if your allowances alter during the year.

The higher your tax code, the lower your tax, unless you have a tax code with a K prefix.

## What do the letters mean?

The letter shown after your tax code defines your status. For example, L = basic personal allowance; P = full personal allowance if aged 65–74 with V being used if you are also entitled to the married couple's allowance and you are on basic rate tax; Y = personal allowance for those aged 75 or over. T is used if there are other items the tax office need to review, or if you have requested that you do not want the identification letter mentioned above to be used.

Codes BR or DO are sometimes used where you have more than one employer or have several sources of income and will mean that you will have tax deducted at basic or higher rate tax. In these cases it is important to check your tax at the year end as there is a danger that you will have overpaid tax and need to claim a refund.

If you do have more than one employment, you can ask the tax office to apportion your personal allowance between the two and your PAYE code number will be altered accordingly.

Sometimes your taxable benefits will exceed your allowances – for example, if you are taxed on car and fuel benefits or private health benefits, or have arrears of tax to collect. In these cases a K code is used so that your employer can recoup this tax on behalf of the tax office.

The tax office may estimate any likely taxable benefits for the 2008–2009 tax year and will probably base them on the latest available figures on their files, which could be quite old if you haven't sent in a tax return for the last couple of years.

You need to check the figures on your PAYE coding notice carefully. If the estimates are excessive, write to your tax office requesting a code change – be sure to quote your NI number and the tax reference.

## Emergency coding

If your employer does not know what tax code to use he will apply an 'emergency' code (543L for 2008–2009 or 522L for 2007–2008); this effectively only gives you the basic personal allowance (regardless of your age) and unless this is your first job the tax system will assume you started work in April, so that you could lose out on any tax-free pay due to you. The quicker you sort out your correct code number, the sooner you will have the correct tax deducted from your earnings.

## How to check your tax code

Nowadays a PAYE coding notice comes in the form of a letter from HMRC and it will explain how your tax code is calculated.

It will certainly start by stating your personal allowance (and, if applicable, the blind person's allowance), to which will be *added* any gift aid payments if you are a higher rate taxpayer, any allowable expenses, any pension payments which have not already had tax relief at the correct rate, and any married couple's allowance or maintenance allowance, although relief on these will be restricted to 10 per cent.

There will be *deductions* for any State pension or taxable State benefits you receive which will have been paid gross, and any benefits you have received from your employer, which will have been detailed in your P11D form, and any casual earnings that you have declared.

Tax underpayments that you had requested in your tax return should be collected via your PAYE code will be taken into account and shown separately.

Ideally, the figures making up your tax code should equate with the figures in your tax return. If they do not, then tell the tax office immediately, otherwise you could end up paying too little or too much tax for the rest of the year.

If your tax code is incorrect, it is more than likely that your previous year's code was also wrong, so that any overpayment of tax is accumulating.

Pay particular attention to any company car and fuel benefits, as following the introduction of new rules, many coding notices have again been issued showing incorrect benefits resulting in unwelcome tax demands at a later date.

Pensioners will often have a tax code applied to any supplementary pension they receive (see Chapter 12 on page 108).

# CHAPTER 11

# How to check your tax

A t the end of the tax year you should check to see if you have paid the correct amount of tax. If you are self-employed you may need to keep a closer eye on your tax affairs during the year and Chapter 13 deals specifically with this.

This chapter is primarily for employees on PAYE, although it will be of interest to all taxpayers as many of the circumstances are not confined just to those on PAYE.

At the end of every tax year, your employer must give you a form P60, which will show how much you have earned in the tax year and, more importantly, how much tax you have paid.

If you receive employee benefits (company car, health insurance, etc.) you will also receive a form P11D (see page 71), which will identify these.

You should check for yourself whether the amount of tax you have paid is correct. This will mean that you need to add up all your income and benefits, deducting allowable expenses (see Chapter 6 on page 78) and any tax allowances, and calculating the tax payable.

If this total tax figure is less than that stated on your P60 form, then you have paid too much tax. Write immediately to your tax office pointing this out and then claim a refund. If you have not paid enough tax, either you or the tax inspector has made a mistake! If you have paid insufficient tax, you are under a legal obligation to send in a tax return so that any outstanding tax can be calculated and paid. The tax office may also adjust your code number so that you do not underpay tax in the following year.

There is a comprehensive chart you can use in the *Check Your Tax* calculator on pages 170–172, but on the next few pages there are simplified examples of how to check your own tax.

In the first example overleaf, Michael is a married man under 65 and the tax calculations are fairly straightforward as he has no savings income or dividends and his income does not take him into the higher rate tax band.

Assuming that these are the figures Michael declared in his 2008 tax return, then the statement he gets from the tax office should agree with his tax calculations and will also confirm that a refund is due. If he had adjustments in his tax code to collect underpayments for earlier tax years, then these would need to be taken into the following calculation.

---

### Example 1: Checking your tax for the year ended 5 April 2008

Michael, who is married and under 65, is employed and had a salary of £27,300 from which his employer had deducted a pension contribution of £750. His employer provided him with a company car and fuel. He did some freelance work at home which, after expenses, gave him £835. He also claimed £115 for professional subscriptions. His tax liability can be summarised as follows:

|  | £ | £ |
|---|---|---|
| Total wages per P60 form | 27,300.00 | |
| Less: Pension contribution | 750.00 | 26,550.00 |
| Casual earnings | | 835.00 |
| Use of company car and fuel benefit, say | | 5,500.00 |
| Total earnings for the year | | 32,885.00 |
| Less: Expenses claimed | | 115.00 |
| Net earnings | | 32,770.00 |
| Less: Personal allowance | | 5,225.00 |
| Total income on which tax is payable | | 27,545.00 |
| Tax payable £ 2,230 at 10 per cent | 223.00 | |
| £25,315 at 22 per cent | 5,569.30 | |
| Tax due | | 5,792.30 |
| Less: Tax paid under PAYE as shown on form P60, say | | 5,900.00 |
| Amount of tax to be claimed back | | £ 107.70 |

---

## The tax office uses a different method

The way in which the above statement was prepared is the normal and simplest way, and the method most accountants would use. Unfortunately, our tax system always makes things as complicated as possible and the statements you receive from the tax office will present the details in a different format. They tend to work backwards, allocating income against tax bands.

However, the net result should be the same and if it is not and you cannot see why there is a difference, write to your tax office and enclose a copy of your workings so they can identify the problems.

## Tax on savings income

For 2007–2008 once the £2,230 income band at 10 per cent has been used, savings income (excluding dividends) is taxed at 20 per cent (not 22 per cent) if you are a basic rate taxpayer; once your income takes you into the higher rate band, then your savings are taxed at 40 per cent.

## Tax on dividends

Just to complicate matters further, dividend income is paid after deducting a tax credit of 10 per cent. Add this credit to the dividend received to give the gross amount to be included in your total income.

For basic rate taxpayers this tax credit covers their tax liability on dividend income, but higher rate taxpayers will be taxed at 32.5 per cent. Dividend income is treated as the top slice of your savings income.

This tax credit cannot be reclaimed if you are a non-taxpayer, nor has it been repayable since 6 April 2004 on shares held in personal equity plans (PEPs) and individual savings accounts (ISAs). Therefore choose investments that pay interest without tax having been deducted before you receive it (see Chapter 18 on page 157) if you are a non-taxpayer.

## Checking your tax

As you will see, the tax system is unnecessarily complicated, but it can be made much simpler to understand if you remember to use the *Check Your Tax* sequence list.

## The *Check Your Tax* sequence list

This is the easy way to calculate your tax for **2007–2008**. It is vital that you do your calculations in the following order:

1. Make a list of your total income under the following headings:

2. **Non savings income and benefits:** First deduct from this your allowances, expenses and pension payments. Then taxed at 10 per cent up to £2,230, then at 22 per cent until the limit of the 22 per cent band is reached (£34,600). Then at 40 per cent thereafter.

3. **Non-dividend savings income:** Taxed at 10 per cent if the £2,230 maximum has not been used up in the above calculation. Then at 20 per cent until the limit of the cumulative 22 per cent band is reached (£34,600). Then at 40 per cent thereafter.

4. **Dividend income:** Taxed at 10 per cent until the limit of the cumulative 22 per cent band is reached. Then at 32.5 per cent.

5. Any taxable life assurance gains or net capital gains are taxable at your highest rate of tax (20 per cent up to £34,600, then 40 per cent).

## Further examples

On page 102 it was explained how Michael, who had a straightforward income structure without any savings income, calculated his tax.

Here are two more examples: Jane, who is a basic rate taxpayer but has savings income; and Alan who is a higher rate taxpayer with savings income and dividends and who also made a gift aid donation during the year.

---

**Example 2: Checking your tax for the year ended 5 April 2008**

In 2007–2008 Jane has a total income *after allowances* of £5,360, which includes £500 interest *received gross*.

She will pay tax on:

|  | £ |  | £ |
|---|---|---|---|
| The first | 2,230 | at 10 per cent | 223.00 |
|  | 2,630 | at the basic rate of 22 per cent | 578.60 |
|  | 500 | at savings rate of 20 per cent | 100.00 |
| Total income | £5,360 | Tax payable | £901.60 |

If Jane had received interest net after tax had been deducted, then the total income would still remain the same, for you must always include the *gross* amount of any income, but the amount of tax payable would be: £901.60 less £100 (20 per cent × £500) being tax already deducted from the interest.

---

**Example 3: Checking your tax for the year ended 5 April 2008**

Alan is married and under 65; he has a salary of £38,500, makes a pension contribution and receives benefits from his employer. He also has casual earnings, interest from a building society and dividends from shares. He also gave £500 to a local charity and signed a gift aid form so, as he is a higher rate taxpayer, he can claim the difference between the basic and higher rate tax rate.

This is how Alan would go about checking his tax liability.

Alan lists his total income, less expenses and allowances, as follows:

|  | £ | £ |
|---|---|---|
| Total salary shown on his P60 form | 38,500.00 |  |
| Less: Pension contribution | 3,800.00 | 34,700.00 |
| Casual earnings |  | 695.00 |
| Use of company car and fuel benefit, say |  | 5,500.00 |
| Total earnings for the year |  | 40,895.00 |
| Less: Expenses claimed |  | 215.00 |
| Net earnings |  | 40,680.00 |
| Less: Personal allowance |  | 5,225.00 |
| **Non-savings income** |  | 35,455.00 |
| Non-dividend savings income received | 432.00 |  |
| Tax deduced at 20 per cent | 108.00 | 540.00 |
| Dividend income received | 450.00 |  |
| Tax credit | 50.00 | 500.00 |
| **Total income** |  | £36,495.00 |

As this total is above the maximum 22 per cent basic rate band of £34,600, Alan is going to be a higher rate taxpayer. Therefore apply the sequence as shown on the previous page to calculate his tax liability as follows.

|  | £ | £ |
|---|---|---|
| **Tax on his non-savings income:** | 2,230.00 at 10 per cent | 223.00 |
|  | 32,370.00 at 22 per cent | 7,121.40 |
| Basic rate band now reached | 34,600.00 |  |
| £35,455–£34,600 | 855.00 at 40 per cent | 342.00 |
| Non-savings income total | 35,455.00 |  |
| **Tax on his non-dividend savings income:** |  |  |
| both the 10 per cent and 22 per cent bands have been fully used above therefore: | £540 at 40 per cent | 216.00 |
| **Tax on his dividend income:** |  |  |
| the 22 per cent band has been fully used above therefore: | £500 at 32.5 per cent | 162.50 |
|  |  | £8,064.90 |
| Less: claim for gift aid donation Gross amount £641 (£500 × $\frac{100}{78}$) at 18 per cent (40%–22%) |  | 115.38 |
|  |  | £7,949.52 |

Alan will already have paid much of this by PAYE deducted from his salary (let's say this was £7,550) and has paid tax by deduction on his interest and dividend income.

So, Alan's final tax bill will be:

| | | |
|---|---|---|
| Tax liability as above | | £7,949.52 |
| Less: Paid under PAYE | £7,550.00 | |
| Deducted from interest | 108.00 | |
| Tax credit on dividend | 50.00 | 7,708.00 |
| Further tax demand to pay | | £  241.52 |

## Income tax repayment claim

If most of the income you receive has already been taxed (for example, interest) it is possible that you can claim back some tax.

Either fill in a self assessment tax return if you have received one or ask for a repayment claim form (form R40), telling your tax office in a covering letter that you think you are due a tax refund.

On form R40 you can claim expenses and deductions in the same way as an ordinary tax return. You do not have to send dividend vouchers and certificates of deduction of tax in support of your claim. However, you should still keep the records as you may be asked to produce evidence at a later date.

Do not forget, when you sign the declaration, that there is another part of the form that you need to sign, which is your legal request for the actual repayment of tax to be made to you.

The following example shows how Joan is due a tax refund and the way it is calculated.

---

### Example 4: Tax repayment for the year 2007–2008

Joan, who is under 65, had a part-time job and earned £3,000, from which tax has not been deducted at source. She also received net interest from a building society of £2,000 (tax deducted £500).

|  | £ | £ |
|---|---|---|
| Earned income | | 3,000.00 |
| Interest received (building society) | 2,000.00 | |
| Tax deducted (i.e. 20 per cent of £2,500) | 500.00 | 2,500.00 |
| Total income | | 5,500.00 |
| Deduct personal allowance | | 5,225.00 |
| Net income | | 275.00 |
| Tax liability: £275 at 10 per cent | | 27.50 |
| Less: tax deducted from interest | | 500.00 |
| Tax refund due | | £ 472.50 |

If Joan had received net *dividend* income of £2,000, instead of building society interest, she would not have been able to reclaim the tax credit that would have been deducted from her dividend.

---

## Tax demands in respect of 2007–2008 income

If your only income is taxed under PAYE, then it is unlikely that you will receive a tax return to complete and, provided you have checked that the right amount of tax had been deducted and your current PAYE tax code is correct, then there is no need to contact your tax office.

If you have other income, or gains, in the year ended 5 April 2008 then you probably need to fill in a tax return. You should complete this and return it to your tax office before 31 October 2008. If you file electronically you have until 31 January 2009.

The tax office will then send you a self assessment tax calculation (form SA 302) showing any sums due (or overpaid).

## Tax payments

Unless you are self-employed, or have sources of untaxed income, most of your tax liability will be paid by PAYE, or by deductions at source, throughout the year; when you send in your tax return, any tax due will be accounted for at the tax year end and is payable by 31 January of the following year.

If you are self-employed, however, or you have income or interest that has not been taxed or you are a higher rate taxpayer with investment income, you may still have to make two payments on account (see page 34).

From time to time your tax office might send you self assessment statements (form SA300) showing you the current position of your tax payments (or refunds). If it is correct, then any tax due must be paid by the date shown; if you disagree with the amount, ask for form SA303 on which you can claim to reduce any payments on account, or write giving your explanation why you think the figures are wrong. You must still pay any tax that you think is due, however, otherwise interest will be charged.

## Interest on late payments and repayments

The tax office will charge you interest on underpayments from the due date but they will pay you interest on overpayments. This is called a repayment supplement and it is not taxable. The interest rate for repayment supplements is currently much lower than the interest rate on underpayments, somewhat unfairly.

# CHAPTER 12

# Pensioners

This chapter applies only to those people who have reached the official retirement age of 65 for men and 60 for women. If you have elected for an earlier retirement you continue to be treated as a taxable individual and you cannot claim the tax concessions available to pensioners until the official retirement age. A married man is entitled to claim the State retirement pension when he reaches 65. On the other hand, if a married woman reaches 60 before her husband is 65, she can only claim the pension if she has paid sufficient national insurance contributions in her own right.

The State retirement pension age for women is to be increased to 65 and is being phased in over a ten-year period between 6 May 2010 and 6 March 2020, so it will start to effect everyone born after 6 April 1950.

Shortly before you reach retirement age you should receive form P161 from your tax office. Fill this in and return it to ensure that you get the correct age allowance and the correct tax code is eventually applied to any pension income you will receive, other than the State pension.

Telephone the Pension Service on 0845 300 1084 if you are four months from retirement and have not had a letter advising you of your pension entitlements. There is also a useful website on **www.the pensionservice.gov.uk**.

If the State pension is going to be your only income then you can apply to your local Department for Work and Pensions office and local council for various benefits to supplement your income; and also consider claiming tax credits (see page 96).

### What to do when you retire

If you have been paying PAYE, you will receive a form P45 from your employer. Send this to the tax office printed on the form, with a letter stating that you have retired, giving the date on which you reached retirement age, details of any pensions you will receive, and stating that you are not intending to take further employment.

Should you later decide to work again, either full time or part time, you will have to ask your tax office for a new tax code.

If you have been self-employed, make sure that your tax returns are up to date and tax liabilities agreed, and inform your tax office of the details of any private pension you will receive.

## Pensions

The State pension, the SERPS supplement and the widow's pension, are taxable, but the Government does not deduct the tax when you receive or collect them. If this State pension is your only source of income, however, then it is unlikely that you will have any tax to pay as your personal allowance will more than cover this income. The war widow's pension is not taxable, neither is the winter fuel payment, nor the Christmas bonus.

## Postponing your State pension

Since 6 April 2005 you have been able to delay taking your State pension for as long as you wish and get either an extra payment added to your pension for each year of postponement, or a lump sum.

Why would you want to postpone? If you have enough income to live on at the moment, then receiving the State pension may put you into either a higher tax bracket or into the age trap scenario (see page 111) and it would be beneficial to delay taking that extra income until perhaps your other income is at a lower level.

You have three options available as regards your State pension entitlements once you reach official retirement age.

1. You can retire and claim your State pension.

2. You can carry on working and claim your State pension.

3. You can delay claiming your State pension – whether you are working or not.

If you decide to delay claiming, you have a further two avenues to consider:

4. You can earn extra State pension that will be added to your normal entitlement when you do decide to claim; the extra amount will be equivalent to 1 per cent of your weekly pension for every five weeks you put off claiming (so 10.4 per cent per year).

or

5. You can claim a one-off lump sum payment based on the amount of State pension you would have received in the period you have put off claiming plus interest; this interest rate will be 2 per cent above the Bank of England's base rate.

You can only opt for the lump sum option if you put off claiming for at least 12 consecutive months.

The phrase 'State pension' includes any earnings-related State pension (SERPS) or S2P (State second pension) and any graduated retirement benefit.

## Tax position on lump sum payment

This lump sum payment needs to be added to your total income for tax purposes, and if this total exceeds your personal allowance you will pay tax on it.

However, the inclusion of any lump sum will only be taxed at the tax rate applicable to your other income; in other words, if you are in the 10 per cent band for 2007–2008 and the addition of a lump sum would take you into the 22 per cent band, the lump sum will only be taxable at 10 per cent.

The pension service will deduct tax from the lump sum payment – you will have to fill in a form stating what you think your total income will be for the year so they can decide what rate of tax to deduct.

Any lump sum will not affect your entitlement to the age-related personal tax allowance. The lump sum will be excluded from your savings total when calculating any savings-credit part of the pension credit.

Even if you are already receiving the State pension you can elect to stop receiving it and adopt one of the above options.

The pension service has published a booklet, *Your State pension choice – Pension now or extra pension later. A guide to State pension deferral*. Telephone 08457 313 233 for a copy.

## Working after retirement

If you carry on working after the official retirement age you can still claim the State pension, although you do not have to pay any more national insurance contributions (employers still have to contribute, however).

Whether you are employed full time or part time, a PAYE tax code will be issued (see page 98) that will tax your earnings.

## Pension credit

This new pension credit was introduced in October 2003 to top up pensioners' income, whilst at the same time rewarding (slightly) those who had saved for their retirement. This replaced the minimum income guarantee. See page 96 for full details to see if you can benefit from making a claim.

## Tax allowances

A husband, wife or civil partner each has their own tax allowance and is responsible for their own tax affairs.

The tax allowances for 2008–2009 are as follows with the 2007–2008 figures in brackets:

| Tax allowances for 2008–2009 | | |
|---|---|---|
| Age for personal allowance | Personal allowance £ | Married couple's allowance £ |
| 65–74 | 9,030 (7,550) | 6,535 (6,285) |
| 75 and over | 9,180 (7,690) | 6,625 (6,365) |

*Notes*
Although the married couple's allowance was abolished from 6 April 2000, it still continues for those couples where either the husband or wife or civil partner was aged 65 or more on or before 5 April 2000 and is based on the age of the *older* of the husband or wife or partner. Relief is restricted to only 10 per cent of the allowance.

However, these age-related personal allowances, as they are called, are reduced if your own total income is above £21,800 (£20,900 for 2007–2008). For every £2 of income above this limit, your allowance is reduced by £1, but no taxpayer can get less than the basic personal allowance of £5,435 (£5,225 for 2007–2008). Similarly, the married couple's allowance will also be reduced by the excess that has not already been taken into account in calculating the reduced personal allowance. Once again, the allowance cannot be reduced below a minimum level – £2,540 for 2008–2009 (£2,440 for 2007–2008).

Don't forget that a wife's income from all sources is considered separately from that of her husband, and similarly for civil partners.

## How to check your tax for 2007–2008

Start by finding out your total income for the year. You must include all your pension income, including the State pension and the gross amount of any interest from banks, building societies, annuities, etc. Also include any dividend income, including the tax credit. You do not have to include any income that is free of tax (see page 13).

Secondly, you need to make a note of any tax that you have already had deducted from your pension or other income. Finally you need to calculate any allowances to which you are entitled.

Remember that if a situation arises where a husband is unable to use part of his married couple's allowance, the balance can be transferred to his wife – ask for Form 575 from your tax office. Similarly with civil partnerships. You have up to five years from 31 January following the tax year in which to make this request.

## Example of how to check your tax for 2007–2008

John, the husband, is aged 73 and his wife, Mary, is 69.

| | | John £ | Mary £ |
|---|---|---|---|
| Income for 2007–2008 | | | |
| State pension, say | | 6,226.00 | 2,850.00 |
| Other pension, gross amount (tax deducted, say £1,500) | | 8,886.00 | |
| Rent from letting unfurnished room (after expenses) | | 4,046.00 | |
| Total non-savings income | | 19,158.00 | 2,850.00 |
| National Saving Bank interest: | | | |
| Ordinary account £40 (the first £70 is not taxable) | | – | |
| Investment account (gross) | | – | 75.00 |
| Bank deposit interest – received | £ 144.00 | | |
| Tax deducted before receipt | 36.00 | 180.00 | |
| Dividend income – received | 1,800.00 | | |
| – tax credit | 200.00 | 2,000.00 | |
| Total income | | 21,338.00 | 2,925.00 |
| Less: Personal allowance | 7,550.00 | | 7,550.00 |
| but restricted because of John's income limit (see note) £21,338–£20,900 = £438 | | | (4,625.00) unused allowance |
| × 50 per cent | 219.00 | 7,331.00 | |
| Taxable income | | £14,007.00 | |

**Now refer to the easy way sequence list on page 103 so that you use the correct percentages in calculating your tax.**

| | | £ |
|---|---|---|
| John's tax liability will be: | | |
| On his non-savings income £19,158 | | |
| Less: his allowances £ 7,331 = £11,827 | | |
| | £2,230 at 10 per cent | 223.00 |
| | £9,597 at 22 per cent | 2,111.34 |
| On his savings income | £180 at 20 per cent | 36.00 |
| On his dividend income | £2,000 at 10 per cent | 200.00 |
| | | 2,570.34 |
| Less: married couple's allowance | £6,285 at 10 per cent | 628.50 |
| Total tax liability | | 1,941.84 |
| But he has already paid by deduction the following amounts of tax: | | |
| On his other pension | £1,500.00 | |
| On his bank interest | 36.00 | |
| On his dividends | 200.00 | 1,736.00 |
| Tax still to pay | | £ 205.84 |

*Notes*
1. John's total income was £21,338; as the income age limit is £20,900 his allowances are reduced by 50 per cent (£1 for every £2 over this limit). This could have been avoided if some of his income-producing assets had been transferred to Mary, his wife.
2. It will be seen that Mary had insufficient income to cover her personal allowance. The unused balance is lost – it cannot be used by her husband. It would have been more sensible for her to have received a greater part of the family income in order to reduce John's tax liability, so they should consider reorganising their investments to avoid the same problem arising next year.
3. Perhaps John should also have let the room furnished instead of unfurnished, with the lodger sharing the house so that the rent could have been received tax free under the rent-a-room scheme (see page 85).

If John and Mary were working out their likely tax situation for 2008–2009 they would still get the married couple's allowance (increased to £6,535). The age income limit would be £21,800 and the basic rate of tax would be 20 per cent, with the lower rate of 10 per cent having been abolished. The personal allowance would also increase to £9,030.

It will still be important for John to transfer some income-bearing investments to his wife, but she should not receive dividends as she cannot reclaim the tax credit if her income remains below her personal allowance; investments paying interest tax free would be preferable (see page 157).

## Income tax repayment

At the end of each tax year on 5 April you should check to see exactly what income you received during the previous year and what tax you have actually paid, as in the above example.

You can get a repayment of tax if you have paid too much. To reclaim tax ask your tax office for leaflet IR110 and a form R40. Complete it in the same way as a tax return (see Chapter 4 on page 21) and send the form to your tax office. There is no need to enclose the dividend and interest vouchers unless the tax office ask for them at a later date.

Where most of your income has already had tax deducted before you receive it (for example, interest) you may be able to make quarterly, half-yearly or annual repayment claims (see page 105).

Even if you are a taxpayer, you may have had tax deducted from interest received at 20 per cent and because you haven't had the benefit of the 10 per cent tax band for 2007–2008 or the 10 per cent savings rate for 2008–2009 (see page 187) you should claim a refund of the difference. There are a great number of pensioners on low incomes who are not making these claims.

## Where to invest your money

In reviewing investments, married and civil partner pensioners in particular should make sure that they are making full use of both personal allowances. They should avoid a situation arising where perhaps one partner is paying tax and the other partner is not using his or her full allowance. To correct such a problem, you should consider switching savings or investments from one to the other.

If you have insufficient income to cover your personal allowances (that is, you are not a taxpayer) it is important to put your savings into investments that do not deduct tax before paying the interest. Otherwise you will only have to cope with more paperwork in claiming the tax back at the end of the year.

In Chapter 18 on page 157 there is a brief summary of the various investment alternatives that are available for savings depending on your circumstances and clarifying whether or not you have to pay tax on the interest or dividends received.

## Building society and bank accounts

A special mention should be made here about these accounts. Many pensioners who may be on low incomes put their savings into building society or bank accounts for safety and convenience. However, tax will be deducted from the interest before you receive it and if you are not a taxpayer (that is, your personal tax allowances exceed your total income) then you should claim the tax back at the end of the year (see page 105). Many people, however, don't realise that *they* have to do this and consequently they are losing out. It is official knowledge that there are many millions of pounds in tax refunds that have not been claimed.

Your bank or building society will pay your interest gross, without deducting tax, if you ask them for a form R85. This is a very simple form to complete and asks you to certify that your total income for the tax year is unlikely to exceed your personal allowances. If you are aged 65 to 74 on 5 April 2008 these figures for 2008–2009 are £9,683 for a married man or civil partner and £9,030 for single people; if you are 75 or more they are £9,842 for a married man or civil partner and £9,180 for single people (assuming an election has not been made to transfer all or part of the married couple's allowance).

You will need your national insurance number to complete this form. If your circumstances change during the tax year and your total income is such that you will become liable to tax, you must inform your bank or building society branch immediately.

## Equity release schemes

With ever-increasing property prices, thousands of pensioners appear to be fairly well off on paper, but in terms of income for everyday living expenses they find it hard to make ends meet. This is where equity release schemes come into play.

Under these schemes you sell all or part of your house for a discounted lump sum and continue to live in it. Or, instead of a lump sum, you can receive a regular income.

There are three main schemes: home reversion schemes, lifetime mortgages and home income plans.

With the first two schemes there are no income tax implications, although clearly the value of your estate, including your house, will reduce the longer the equity release scheme stays in place and this might reduce any inheritance tax liability; on the other side of the coin, you will be reducing the value of any inheritance that you may wish to pass on to children, relatives or friends when you die.

With these two schemes it is important that you approach several firms for quotations, use an independent solicitor (not one recommended by the scheme itself) and ensure that you have the greatest degree of flexibility if your circumstances change and you want to terminate the scheme or move house.

With home income plans, instead of receiving a lump sum as with the above schemes, you can elect to take an annuity in order to give you an ongoing income. (See below for the tax implications.)

## Purchased life annuities

Do not confuse these with annuities you purchase with a pension fund. These are taxed quite differently.

When you receive an annuity payment it consists of two elements: capital and income. The capital portion is non-taxable but the insurance company will deduct tax from the income portion (which you must enter on your tax return) and provide you with a tax deduction certificate, which you will need in order to claim any tax repayment. Tax will be deducted at the basic rate of 22 per cent for 2007–2008 and 20 per cent for 2008–2009. You will not get any tax relief on buying the actual annuity.

Annuities are particularly useful if you have no dependants or your children or relatives do not need additional assets.

Bear in mind that any extra income from an annuity could reduce any means-tested social security benefit, could affect your age-related personal allowance and will not take inflation into account in succeeding years. Also, you cannot cancel an annuity and get your capital back.

## Pre-1999 annuity

Provided at least 90 per cent of the lump sum received on mortgaging your house was used to buy the annuity and the loan was taken out before 9 March 1999, then the interest on a mortgage of up to £30,000 will be tax deductible at the basic rate, even though mortgage interest tax relief was abolished for other loans from 6 April 2000. You had to be 65 or over at 9 March 1999.

## Your pension scheme retirement options

If you are a member of your employer's pension scheme or have a personal pension scheme of your own, it is important to consider all the options when you retire.

On your retirement, a tax-free cash lump sum payment is normally available, the calculation of which depends on the type of scheme.

If you are a member of your employer's final salary occupational pension scheme, your lump sum calculation will depend on your years of service and taxable earnings (including P11D benefits) at retirement. You should ask your insurance company or scheme administrator for this information; money purchase schemes have different rules.

As from 6 April 2006, the provisions of the new pensions legislation took effect, which endeavoured to simplify the existing complicated tax legislation (see page 165) regarding the rules and the way in which you get tax relief for your pension contributions.

When you are considering your pension rights both as regards tax-free lump sum payments and income options, do ensure that you get detailed quotes, not only from your current pension scheme provider, but also from other companies. This is known as your open-market option – you do not have to stay with your existing company.

From a tax point of view, remember that your pension income has to be added to your State pension and all your other income to arrive at your total income for tax purposes, and this figure will determine what PAYE tax code will be applied to your pension income, for the provider of your pension will deduct tax before paying your pension.

Two useful reference sources are the Office of the Pension Advisory Service (OPAS) – their website is **www.opas.org.uk**; and there is a helpline specifically for women on 0845 600 0806.

In spite of the simplification of the new pension legislation, the various pension options are still a minefield, so do ensure that you get professional advice.

## The two main options on retirement

Only a general overview is given here so it is important to consult a professional advisor.

### Option one

Use your pension fund, less any cash lump sum taken, to buy a lifetime annuity but remember that on your death there will be no capital sum to pass on to your family unless your annuity contract guarantees a certain capital sum or it is 'value protected' in some way.

### Option two

Leave your pension fund intact and draw an income as you need it – this used to be called 'income drawdown' but is now referred to as an 'unsecured pension' under the new pension legislation.

However, if you reach the age of 75, you do need to consult a pension adviser on how much pension you can secure within the new tax limits (both as regards alternatively secured pensions (ASP) and the new open annuity (NDA) options); also the impact of any possible inheritance tax on any pension funds remaining on your death, although partly to mitigate a liability here it has been confirmed in the 2008 budget that the percentage of a partner's unutilised inheritance tax exemption limit on death is not lost but can effectively be transferred to a surviving partner to increase their exemption limit.

# CHAPTER 13

# Self-employed

A self-employed person is one who owns a business or is in partnership with someone else. If you trade as a limited company, you, as a director, are an employee and not self-employed.

## Advantages over PAYE

Self-employed people do not pay PAYE – this method of collecting tax is strictly for employees; instead they pay tax on their profits under what is called Schedule D.

There are definite advantages in paying tax under Schedule D as there are more opportunities for self-employed people to reduce their tax bill than an employed person. There are more expenses that can be claimed and they are somewhat easier to claim. In addition, there is loss relief which can be set against other taxable income or, in the early years of a business, can be carried back against your total income for the previous three years.

If you are self-employed, you may find it more convenient to deal with the paperwork and meet some of your business contacts at your home. This, in effect, becomes a second place of business, so that you can claim against your profits a proportion of your household expenses, such as heating and lighting.

## Start off on the right lines

1. When you start a new business, you must tell your tax office within three months of starting, otherwise you could face a fine of £100.

   You also need to notify the NI contributions office so that you do not build up arrears of NI contributions or miss out on benefits. The tax office issues a booklet *Starting your own business* CWL1, which has useful advice and a form which can be used to notify the relevant departments that you have started trading. There is a helpline for the newly self-employed on 0845 915 4515.

2. You might have a tax liability in the first year, unless you make a loss, or your profit is offset by allowances or reliefs. Do not wait for the tax office to send you a tax return – ask for one.

3. You may have been employed before starting up in business on your own. If so, you should send the P45 form you will have received from your previous employer to your local tax office and you may be able to claim a tax refund immediately.

4. If you do not use your own name, you must show the names and addresses of the owners of the business on business letters, orders, invoices, receipts and demands for payment. You must also display the names and addresses at your business premises.

5. It may be advantageous to take your wife, husband or civil partner in as a business partner if not already employed elsewhere. However, it should be borne in mind that both partners become jointly and severally liable for the partnership debts, which might put family assets, including your house, in jeopardy. Also in the case of divorce, the business could be seriously affected. Do not forget that, depending on earnings levels and share of profits, there might be a liability to pay tax and national insurance contributions (see Chapter 14 on page 130).

6. When you are in a partnership it is advisable to have a written agreement setting out its terms, particularly if your wife or husband is a partner.

7. You should open a separate bank account for your business which, in the case of a partnership, should be in the partnership names.

8. Keep books detailing your business dealings: the minimum you should keep are a cash book for all monies received and paid, an analysis book for purchases and one for sales, and a petty cash book for miscellaneous expenses.

   It is essential that you keep all purchase invoices and copy sales invoices, not only for the purpose of preparing your accounts but also to keep a check on the amounts you may have to pay and charge in respect of value added tax.

9. Check your turnover – should you register for VAT? The turnover limits above which you must register are £67,000 for 2008–2009 (£61,000 for 2007–2008). The de-registration limits are £2,000 less than these figures. The standard rate for VAT is 17.5 per cent.

10. Always bear in mind that both the tax inspector and the VAT inspector have a legal right to require you to supply evidence from your books and records for any particular year. Under self assessment you must keep books and records for five years and ten months from the end of the tax year.

11. Make regular provision for a retirement pension (see page 166).

12. If you run your business from your own house then do bear in mind that there may be a capital gains tax liability (see page 141). Also check the council tax situation.

13. Check your insurances – advise your insurers if you are operating from your home address or using your own car.

14. Consider establishing a limited liability partnership (LLP), the main purpose of which is to protect partners from excessive claims against the partnership.

## How are you taxed?

Many self-employed people think you pay tax only on what you take out of the business for yourself as drawings or wages. This is not so. Drawings are sums taken on account of the profit you expect to make. You are taxed on your total profit before deducting any drawings.

To find out how much profit you have made, prepare an account showing your total business income less your business expenses. This is not necessarily the figure on which your tax is calculated, for you have to add any disallowable items mentioned below.

It is this amended profit figure, not the one shown in your accounts, that you should enter in your tax return. Your claim for capital allowances must also be entered (see page 126). This adjustment and claim for capital allowances is called a tax computation.

Refer to the actual *Self-employed* supplementary tax return pages reproduced on page 39; also the *Partnership* pages on page 42.

## Allowable expenses and deductions

Apart from your normal business expenses (such as purchase of goods, rent, rates, staff wages) you should consider claiming the following:

- Hotel and travelling expenses on business trips – not forgetting part of the total running expenses of your car.

- The business usage part of your private telephone bill.

- Bank interest and charges on your business account.

- Business subscriptions and magazines.

- Special clothing necessary for your type of business, including cleaning costs, etc.

- Bad and doubtful debts that can be specifically identified.

- Gifts advertising your business (but the cost must not exceed £50 per person, and must not be food, drinks, tobacco or vouchers).

- Repairs and renewals to business property (for example, the cost of replacing a shopfront, less any part of that cost representing any improvement).

- Employer's national insurance contributions on employee's wages and benefits (see page 131 for your own NIC deductions).

## Expenses and deductions not allowable

It is possible that your business payments include some expenses which are not allowable for tax. In this case, your profit must be increased so as to exclude this private element. Examples of the more usual items are a proportion of:

- Rent, light, heat and council tax – where you live in part of the business premises (for example, a flat above your shop).

- Motor car expenses, including hire purchase interest, where you use a business car for private journeys.

- Telephone bills.

And the whole of:

- Depreciation on all assets, if included in your accounts, whether they are business or private. You can instead claim capital allowances (see page 125).

- Capital expenditure – the cost of computers, cars, machinery, etc. – or expenditure involving improvement as distinct from the repair of an asset. Instead, claim capital allowances where possible.

- Entertaining either UK or overseas customers.

- Your own earnings.

- Class 2 and Class 4 NICs (see page 133).

- Donations to political parties and charitable donations that do not directly benefit your business.

## Example of business accounts and a tax computation

It has been assumed that John Wiltshire has been in business for several years, as there are special rules for new businesses.

### John Wiltshire – Florists
### Profit and loss account for year ended 5 April 2008

| | £ | | £ |
|---|---:|---|---:|
| Opening stock | 750 | Sales or takings | 79,200 |
| Purchases | 22,000 | Closing stock | 2,500 |
| Gross profit | 58,950 | | |
| | £81,700 | | £81,700 |
| Staff wages and NIC | 6,842 | Gross profit | 58,950 |
| Rent and rates | 14,126 | Rent receivable | 750 |
| Telephone | 427 | Profit on sale of | |
| Light and heat | 623 | motor car | 398 |
| Legal fees re new lease | 100 | Interest received (gross) | 105 |
| Insurance of shop | 181 | | |
| Motor expenses | 512 | | |
| Travelling/entertaining | 107 | | |
| Postage and stationery | 87 | | |
| General expenses | 202 | | |
| Bank charges and interest | 64 | | |
| Depreciation: | | | |
| Motor car | 600 | | |
| Fixtures | 376 | | |
| Repairs and renewals | 789 | | |
| Wife's wages | 980 | | |
| Own wages | 20,000 | | |
| Own NIC | 278 | | |
| | 46,294 | | |
| Net profit | 13,909 | | |
| | £60,203 | | £60,203 |

Although John Wiltshire will start with these accounts, various adjustments will have to be made to arrive at an adjusted profit for tax purposes. A tax computation based on the accounts will have to be prepared as shown opposite:

# John Wiltshire – Florists
## Profit adjusted for income tax for year ended 5 April 2008

|  | £ | £ |
|---|---:|---:|
| Profit per accounts |  | 13,909 |
| Less: Income taxed separately: |  |  |
|     Rent received | 750 |  |
|     Interest received gross | 105 |  |
|     Profit on sale of motor car | 398 |  |
|  |  | 1,253 |
|  |  | 12,656 |
| Add: Items not allowable for tax purposes: |  |  |
|     Own wages and NIC | 20,278 |  |
|     Repairs and renewals – new till | 525 |  |
|     Depreciation: Motor car | 600 |  |
|              Fixtures | 376 |  |
|     General expenses – donations | 22 |  |
|     Entertaining customers | 66 |  |
|     Motor expenses – 20 per cent private use | 102 |  |
|     Legal fees re new lease | 100 |  |
|  |  | 22,069 |
|  |  | 34,725 |

|  | £ | £ | £ |
|---|---:|---:|---:|
| Less: Capital allowances |  | 1,100 |  |
|     Less: Private use of car | £ 220 |  |  |
|         Balancing charge re motor car | 144 |  |  |
|  |  | 364 |  |
|  |  |  | 736 |
| Taxable profit |  |  | £ 33,989 |

(Note: the detail of the capital allowances and balancing charge is not shown above.)

---

### John Wiltshire – Florists
### Tax computataion

John Wiltshire's tax liability is as follows for 2007–2008:

| | | |
|---|---:|---:|
| Taxable profit (as above) | | £ 33,989 |
|    Deduct: Personal pension (note 1) | | 1,820 |
| | | 32,169 |
|    Rent | £750 | |
|    Interest received gross | 105 | 855 |
| | | 33,024 |
|    Deduct: Personal allowance | | 5,225 |
| Taxable income | | £ 27,799 |
| | | |
|    Total income tax payable | | |
|    £ 2,230 at 10 per cent | | 223.00 |
|    £    105 at 20 per cent (savings) | | 21.00 |
|    £ 25,464 at 22 per cent | | 5,602.08 |
|    £ 27,799 | | 5,846.08 |
|    Add tax relief at source on pension contribution (note 1) | | 400.00 |
|    Class 4 NIC payable: £34,840 (max) – £5,225 (lower limit) | | |
|      = £29,615 at 8 per cent | | 2,369.20 |
| Total tax and NIC | | £ 8,615.28 |

*Notes*

1. All contributions to personal pension plans are payable net of basic rate tax. John would have deducted tax of £400.00 before paying the contributions.
2. If Mrs Wiltshire's wages are going to be her only income next year, she will lose part of her own personal allowance if they stay at their current low level. It would be more tax advantageous to increase her wages to utilise her full allowance and thus reduce the tax paid by John on his profits.
3. John will make payments on account of his tax and NIC liability on 31 January and 31 July 2008, paying (or receiving) any balance on 31 January 2009.
4. If John's taxable profit had exceeded £34,840 he would have paid an extra 1 per cent on the excess in NI contributions.

## Pension contributions

Refer to page 166.

## Capital allowances

You should set aside part of your profits to save for the replacement of those assets which either become worn out or obsolete. This provision would be shown as depreciation in your accounts.

As mentioned in the previous section, your depreciation provisions are ignored for tax purposes and instead you can claim capital allowances (see table opposite) as a tax deduction.

Special apportionment rules apply when a business begins or ceases.

Remember that you can claim capital allowances on assets that you transfer to the business when you start up (such as furniture, car, etc.).

If you use a business asset for private purposes – for instance, a motor car for the weekends and holidays – you must reduce the allowances by the proportion representing your private use.

If one year's business profit was small enough to be covered by your tax allowances, or you had suffered a trading loss so that you pay no tax, then it may be more worthwhile for you *not* to claim the whole of the capital allowances; this would keep the written down value for tax purposes higher to give you larger writing down allowances to set against your future profits.

### Buying plant and machinery

It is normally better to buy plant or equipment on the last day of one financial year rather than the first day of your next year – the reason being that you get the equivalent of a full year's capital allowance even though you have owned it for only a matter of hours and, although legally yours, have not necessarily paid for it. You need not pay the whole purchase price, but you can buy on hire purchase.

### Selling plant and machinery

All plant and machinery eligible for a writing down allowance (other than cars costing £12,000 or more and other assets with an element of private use) is 'pooled' and on any sale you only have to deduct any proceeds of sale before calculating the writing down allowance. If the proceeds exceed the total value of the pool, after adding the additions for the year, the excess will be charged to tax as a balancing charge. On cars costing £12,000 or more, the maximum allowance is £3,000 a year. Assets used in part privately also have to be grouped in separate pools.

With any other asset, if you expect to dispose of it within two years for less than the tax written down value, you can elect within two years of the year of acquisition to 'depool' the asset. On disposal, the difference between the tax written down value at that date and the proceeds, if less, will be allowed as an extra relief (known as a balancing allowance) or, if more, charged to tax as a balancing charge.

It was announced in the March 2008 budget that 'pools' with a remaining value of up to £1,000 can be written off against profits.

| Capital allowances | | |
|---|---|---|
| | 2007–2008 % | 2008–2009 % |
| **Plant and machinery** | | |
| First year allowance (see note 1) | 40 | – |
| Annual investment allowance (maximum £50,000 a year) | – | 100 |
| Annual writing down allowance on reducing balance | 25 | 20 |
| **Motor cars** | | |
| First year allowance for cars with $CO_2$ emissions not exceeding 120g/km | 100 | 100 |
| Annual writing down allowance on reducing balance on all other cars (maximum £3,000 a year) | 25 | 20 |

*Notes:*

1. Small businesses can claim 50 per cent. To qualify, the business must satisfy two out of three conditions: have a turnover of less than £5.6 million, have assets of less than £2.8 million, have less than 50 employees.

2. There are 100 per cent first year allowances available on certain environmentally friendly equipment and he renovation of business premises.

3. You can claim a 4 per cent writing down allowance on factories, warehouses, agricultural and hotel buildings and houses under assured tenancies schemes.

4. From April 2008, a writing down allowance of 10 per cent is available on assets with a working life of 25 years or more (previously 6 per cent).

5. The list of assets that have special capital allowances is now fairly extensive; for a full list log on to **www.hmrc.gov.uk**.

## Your tax assessments

### For existing businesses

Profits are assessed to tax based on the accounts year ending during the tax year; for example, accounts made up for the year ended 30 June 2007 would be the basis for the 2007–2008 computation, those made up to 5 April 2007 would be for 2006–2007.

### For new businesses

The date to which you prepare accounts is entirely up to you. Special rules of assessment apply for the first two tax years. For example, if your first accounts are for year ended 30 June 2007, your tax computations will be based as follows:

1. Year one 2006–2007: On the profit earned between the 1 July 2006 starting date and 5 April 2007 (apportioned on a time basis).

2. Year two 2007–2008: On the profit earned for the first 12 months of trading (that is year ended 30 June 2007.)

3. Year three 2008–2009: On the accounts for the year ended 30 June 2008.

As you will see in the above example, part of the first year's profits are taxed twice in years one and two (1 July 2006 to 5 April 2007). This is referred to as the overlap profit and details should be kept of the overlapping period and profit, as you are able to claim overlap relief if your business ceases or, in certain circumstances, you change the date to which you draw up your accounts.

## Your tax bills

You pay tax on your adjusted profit less capital allowances, personal allowances and deductions you will have claimed in your tax return.

Your total tax bill is normally payable in two equal instalments on 31 January and 31 July in each year, to which is added any Class 4 national insurance contributions (see page 133). Any tax that has been deducted from trading income (other than subcontractors in the construction industry) can be offset.

If you are in a partnership, the partnership profits will still need to be agreed in the firm's name and no partner can independently agree just his or her own share of the profits. However, the tax liability for each partner will be calculated separately, taking into account each partner's personal allowances and reliefs. Partners are no longer responsible for the other partners' tax liabilities.

## Trading losses

If you should make a loss it can be deducted from the following in the order that saves you most tax:

1. Other income, and then any capital gains, of the same tax year.

2. Other income, and then any capital gains, of the previous year.

3. Trading profits of future years.

4. Any income in the preceding three tax years, provided the loss arises in the first four tax years of a business, but note that losses are set against the earliest years first.

5. Any profits over the previous three tax years if the loss arises in the last 12 months before closing down.

You cannot claim all your tax reliefs and only a part of any loss; you must claim the whole of the loss first. Therefore before making a claim for loss relief, you should calculate whether you would lose a significant proportion of your personal allowances and deductions.

If, after deducting the loss as suggested above, you find that the remaining income is insufficient to cover your personal allowances, it may be better to carry forward the whole loss with a view to setting it off against future profits from the same trade.

## National insurance contributions

Another liability you have while running your own business is national insurance contributions. Refer to Chapter 14 on page 130 for details.

## Selling up or retiring?

Whether you sell the business, retire, or stop trading for any other reason, you could be faced with revised tax liabilities as profits are assessed differently in the closing years. Refer also to Chapter 15 on page 134 for any capital gains tax exposure.

## Post cessation receipts

If you receive monies after a business has been discontinued and tax assessments have been finalised, you must declare such income in the *Additional information* pages (see page 62) in your tax return. Any 'late' relevant expenditure can be offset against such receipts for tax purposes or shown separately (see page 60).

If your other income in the year of payment of post cessation expenses is not sufficient to utilise the relief in full, then a claim can be made for the excess to be treated as an allowable loss for capital gains purposes.

## Employed or self-employed?

To establish whether you are employed or self-employed for tax purposes will depend on a number of factors, most notably whether an individual invests in his or her business, risks capital, provides substantial equipment and materials and/or works for a fixed number of hours at another's premises under the direction of a third party – or is free to come and go as they please and, possibly, have a number of clients.

The new rules have been in existence since 6 April 2000. Each case is judged on its merits and the tax office will give an opinion if asked. The website at **www.hmrc.gov.uk** will give you further information.

## Managed service companies

The tax authorities are seeking to treat workers who provide their services via an intermediary such as a service company, and enter into working arrangements with clients which have the characteristics of employment, as an employee of that client for tax and NIC purposes.

The tax authorities are concerned at the loss of revenue by virtue of the fact that, for instance, the service company can invoice the client without deducting PAYE or national insurance contributions and the worker can then take money out of the company in the form of, say, dividends rather than salary, thus avoiding NICs and gaining other tax advantages.

Several test cases are still being explored through the courts.

Provisions exist for HMRC to charge corporation tax on dividends and distributions paid to non-company shareholders by close companies; this was designed to counteract the situation that arose whereby individuals have transferred their business to a limited company to take advantage of the nil rate band of corporation tax that existed in earlier years.

Since April 2006, however, the nil rate of corporation tax has been abolished and normal corporation tax rates have applied to all profits.

New definitions of managed service companies were introduced and there are provisions to compel such companies to operate PAYE and Class 1 national insurance on all payments received by individuals in respect of services provided through such companies.

# CHAPTER 14

# National insurance

Unless you can get exemption on the grounds of low earnings, old age or incapacity, everyone has to pay national insurance contributions on earnings from your employment or profits from being self-employed. It is compulsory and therefore a further tax on income.

## National insurance contributions

By law, all employers have to deduct a national insurance contribution (NIC) from an employee's pay over a certain limit and pass it on to the tax office, together with the employer contribution. National insurance contributions are levied on your earnings over certain limits and are not allowed as a deduction for tax purposes.

'Earnings' for NIC purposes include pay, bonuses, fees, benefits, etc. and any non-business payments made by your employer on your behalf.

There are lower scales of NI contributions for employees who have contracted out of the State pension scheme and who are members of an approved employer's scheme.

There are six types of national insurance contribution:

1. **Class 1.** Earnings-related contributions payable by most employees, including directors. Employers also have to pay a contribution.

2. **Class 1A.** Payable by the employer on most benefits paid to employees.

3. **Class 1B.** Payable by employers for PAYE settlement agreements.

4. **Class 2.** A flat rate payable by self-employed persons.

5. **Class 3.** If, for some reason, your contribution record under Classes 1 and 2 is inadequate for you to qualify for some NI benefits, you can pay voluntary contributions to make up your record.

6. **Class 4.** Earnings-related contributions payable by self-employed persons and assessed at the same time as income tax. These payments are in addition to Class 2 contributions.

You are exempt from paying Class 4 contributions for 2008–2009 if, on 6 April 2008, you are a man aged 65 (or a woman aged 60) or over or if you are under 16 or you are non-resident for tax purposes. There are also exemptions if you are infirm.

A table giving all the rates for 2008–2009 is reproduced on page 133. Refer to Appendix 4 on page 184 for the 2007–2008 rates.

The NI contributions office have a helpline for employees on 0191 225 7447 and for employers on 08457 143143.

If you have more than one employer or both employment and self-employment income, then at the end of the year you can claim back any national insurance deductions made in excess of the annual maximum by writing to the NICO Refunds Group at Longbenton, Newcastle upon Tyne NE98 1ZZ.

## NICs on company benefits

Where taxable benefits are given to employees (see page 71), then any amounts taxable on individuals and shown on their P11D forms are liable to employer's Class 1A national insurance contributions at 12.8 per cent. This additional NIC liability is payable by the employer annually in arrears in July.

The tax office issue a free guide (CWG5) which shows those benefits that are liable and those that are exempt from this NI charge. Those that are liable are also shown on the P11D form (see page 71).

## Contracting out

There are lower scales of NI contributions for employees who have contracted out of the State earnings-related pension scheme (see overleaf) and who are members of an approved employer's scheme.

Individuals may also contract out via an appropriate personal pension scheme and have a proportion of both their employer's and their own national insurance contributions, referred to as the contracted-out rebate, paid into their own personal pension plan.

## Self-employed

All self-employed people are liable to pay flat rate Class 2 NICs either by a direct payment or direct debit through a bank, etc.

If your earnings from self-employment in 2008–2009 are going to be less than £4,825 (£4,635 in 2007–2008) you may apply at the local tax office to be exempted on the grounds of small earnings.

Inform the tax office if Class 2 contributions are not due for any period (for example, if you are incapacitated). Alternatively, as the contributions are now set at the low rate of £2.30 per week, you may prefer to continue to pay Class 2 and thereby maintain your record of contributions.

In addition, you may be liable to pay a Class 4 contribution based on your profits chargeable to tax after deducting any capital allowances.

If, in addition to running your own business, you also have earnings from an employment on which you pay PAYE tax, then you may be liable to pay additional Class 1 national insurance contributions. However, there is an upper limit on your total liability – ask your tax office for an explanatory booklet or telephone the helpline on 08459 154655. New businesses can contact 0845 915 4515.

In these circumstances you may be eligible to apply for a deferral of Class 4 NI contributions rather than wait to claim a refund at the end of the year. However, deferment will only apply to the main NI rate and you will still be liable at the 1 per cent rate on all profits over the upper limit.

An application for deferral or exemption has to be done annually and there are strict time limits.

## Married women

If you are paying reduced national insurance rates, it may be beneficial for you to cancel this election if you are below the minimum earning level – that way you will not have to pay national insurance but could still build up entitlement to benefits.

In calculating a wife's pension, the number of years of contributions is relevant – women need 39 qualifying years – but:

- You can make voluntary contributions (Class 3) backdated to April 1996.

- Home responsibilities protection (HRP) (for example, at home looking after children or getting income support because you are caring for a disabled person) does not give you a credit on your pension record, but reduces the number of qualifying years.

  This is probably not in any pension forecast that you may get from the pension service (see page 168) as it is not given automatically, so do challenge the figures if you have been involved in HRP.

## National insurance rates and limits for 2008–2009

| | |
|---|---|
| **Class 1** employed earner<br>**Standard rate**<br>for non-contracted out employees | **Employees**<br>11 per cent on earnings above £105 a week up to and including earnings of £770 a week, then 1 per cent on all earnings above this figure |
| | **Employers**<br>12.8 per cent on earnings above £100 a week |
| **Class 1A**<br>On most benefits given to employees | 12.8 per cent payable only by employers based on individual's assessable benefit (see page 66) |
| **Class 1B**<br>PAYE settlement agreements | 12.8 per cent payable by employers |
| **Class 2 Self-employed**<br>Small earnings exemption | £2.30 a week<br>£4,825 a year |
| **Class 3**<br>Voluntary contributions rate | £8.10 a week |
| **Class 4 Self-employed** | 8 per cent between £5,435 and £40,040 and 1 per cent thereafter |
| Lower limit of profits<br>Upper limit of profits | £5,435<br>£40,040 |

*Notes*
There are lower percentages for contracted-out employees and reduced rates for certain married women and widows holding a certificate of election (CF383), share fishermen and volunteer development workers.

## More than one NI number?

The number of employees that seem to have more than one national insurance number seems to be increasing and it is obviously a worry in that you might miss out on having an accurate payment record and this may affect your benefit entitlement – particularly to the State pension. If you are in this position, write to the Account Investigation Section, Banburgh House, Room BP1002, Benton Park View, Longbenton, Newcastle upon Tyne NE98 1ZZ.

# CHAPTER 15

# Capital gains tax

The earlier chapters in this book dealt with tax that may be payable on income (that is, your earnings, pensions, investment income, etc.).

You may also be liable to pay tax on gains from assets and possessions, for example, land and buildings, shares, antiques, paintings or a business, when such assets change hands.

The taxation of capital gains has always been complicated. Therefore, only a concise summary is given here in order to provide background knowledge. If in doubt, seek professional advice.

This chapter deals specifically with disposals by individuals. There are special rules for business assets (but see page 139) and interests in trusts, which are outside the scope of this book.

## What is a capital gain?

A capital gain is any profit arising when you sell, transfer, give, receive compensation for, or otherwise dispose of any of your assets or possessions. There is no capital gains tax payable on death but instead your estate may be liable to pay inheritance tax (see Chapter 16 on page 142).

## Is there such a thing as a capital loss?

Yes; obviously it is the reverse of a capital gain, and any capital losses are deducted from any capital gains that you make in the same year. If your capital losses exceed your capital gains, then you cannot claim tax back, but you can carry forward the losses against future gains.

## Assets that are exempted from capital gains

The most important asset for most people will be your own house. If it is owned and occupied by you and is your main residence, this is *free of capital gains tax* – but see pages 79 and 140 if it is part-let or used for business. Thus a husband and wife, and same-sex couples who have entered into a statutory civil registration from 5 December 2005, can have only one main residence between them; a couple who co-habit can have one residence each and are thus technically in a more favourable position tax wise.

Perhaps the second most important exemption is transfers of assets between married couples and civil partners. These are treated as taking place for no capital profit or loss; this does not apply if the parties are separated or divorced.

Other exempted assets are:

- Chattels – such as jewellery, pictures and furniture – where the proceeds are £6,000 or less; if the proceeds exceed £6,000, the gain is the lower of the proceeds less cost, or proceeds less £6,000 multiplied by 5/3 (this limit has remained at this level since 1970!).

- Child trust funds.

- Compensation for personal or professional injury.

- Decorations for gallantry, unless purchased.

- Foreign currency for personal use.

- Gambling, pools and lottery winnings and prizes.

- Gifts to amateur sports clubs open to the whole community.

- Gifts of outstanding public interest given to the nation.

- Gifts to charities.

- Government stocks and public corporation stocks.

- A house owned and occupied by you which is your main residence. If part let, see page 140, and for claims for use of your home as your office see page 79.

- Individual savings accounts (ISAs), including the transfer of shares from an employee share scheme; and TESSA accounts.

- Interests in certain settled property.

- Land and buildings given to the National Trust.

- Life policies and deferred annuities (unless sold on by original owner).

- Motor cars (private).

- National Savings investments; premium bonds.

- Pension plans (registered).

- Personal equity plan (PEP) investments held for at least a full calendar year, starting 1 January.

- Qualifying corporate bonds.

- Save as You Earn schemes.

- Shares subscribed for under the business expansion scheme (BES) or enterprise investment scheme (EIS).

- Shares subscribed for in approved quoted venture capital trusts.

- Wasting assets with a likely life of 50 years or less.

## Annual exemption

You are allowed to make capital gains of £9,600 (£9,200 in 2007–2008) in each year (after deducting capital losses) before you are liable to pay capital gains tax. Most trusts are exempt on the first £4,800 (£4,600 in 2007–2008).

In addition, there may also be relief for inflation prior to April 2008, depending on how long you have held an asset (see below).

## How to avoid capital gains tax

The main step to take is to ensure that you are making full use of the 'free of tax' list above. For example, do put some of your savings into ISAs, pension schemes, National Savings, Government stocks and various enterprise schemes.

If you do hold shares and other assets that can be readily sold, manage them in such a way that you take advantage of the annual exemption amounts.

Married couples and civil partners each get the annual exemption in their own right, but losses cannot be offset between husband and wife, nor between partners.

Transfers of assets made between married couples and civil partners are treated as taking place for no capital gain or loss if they are living together. This does not apply if the parties are separated or divorced.

## Rates of tax

Prior to 6 April 2008, an individual paid capital gains tax on gains above the annual exemption limit at income tax rates as if the gains were savings added to total income. You may therefore have been liable to capital gains tax at the starting rate (10 per cent), savings rate (20 per cent) or higher rate (40 per cent) depending on your other income

From 6 April 2008, all the above rates will be replaced by a flat rate of 18 per cent on all personal capital gains (see page 139 for business assets).

## Relief for inflation prior to 6 April 2008

In respect of assets held at 5 April 1998, an indexation allowance can be claimed for the period of ownership up to 30 April 1998. Thereafter a tapering relief system applied to those assets and to assets purchased after 5 April 1998.

### Indexation allowance

The indexation is based on the value at 31 March 1982, or acquisition value if acquired later, so you will need to know the value at 31 March 1982 for assets acquired before then. Refer to your tax office to obtain the percentage by which the retail prices index has increased either from 31 March 1982, or the date you acquired the asset (if later), to April 1998.

Note that indexation can only be offset against any capital gain; it cannot be used to create or increase a capital loss.

### Tapering relief

A tapering scale replaced the indexation allowance from 6 April 1998 (see table on page 138). Assets acquired before 17 March 1998 qualified for an addition of one year when applying the taper (except

---

### Example of the combination of indexation allowance and tapering relief on assets sold prior to 6 April 2008

A non-business asset costing £10,000 in 1989 and sold for £20,000, after deducting allowable selling costs, in March 2005.

| | £ | £ |
|---|---|---|
| Disposal proceeds | | 20,000 |
| Cost | 10,000 | |
| Indexation allowance from 1989 to 1998 | | |
| based on Inland Revenue index, say | 4,000 | 14,000 |
| Gain before taper relief | | £ 6,000 |

Tapering relief*: seven years' taper relief (see chart on page 135) means that the gain of £6,000 is reduced to 75 per cent × £6,000, giving a chargeable gain of £4,500. (*Six years plus one extra year, as the asset was held prior to 17 March 1998.)

This is less than the annual exemption amount (£8,200 for 2004–2005), so there will be no capital gains tax liability if this was the only sale in the year.

*Notes*
1. If the asset had been held prior to 31 March 1982, the value at that date would have been used as the cost if it was higher than the original cost.
2. If you elect to re-base the cost of an asset to its 1982 value, all chargeable assets have to be valued that way; you cannot be selective.

for business assets disposed of on or after 6 April 2000).

The taper is applied to the net gains that are chargeable after the deduction of any current year's losses and losses brought forward from earlier years. The annual exemption amount will then be deducted from the tapered gains.

Remember to restrict losses brought forward to an amount that does not bring your chargeable gain below the annual exemption, otherwise this will be wasted.

Purchases and sales within a 30-day period are matched so that no gain or loss will be realised for tax purposes, therefore the practice known as 'bed and breakfasting' has become redundant.

### What is the cost of an asset?
For assets purchased or acquired since 31 March 1982, the initial purchase price (or market value if not purchased), plus acquisition expenses incurred before indexation is applied, will be the cost figure for calculating any capital gain or loss.

For assets held before 31 March 1982 you can use either their original cost (or market value if not purchased) plus expenses, or the

| Capital gains tapering relief chart for assets prior to 6 April 2008 | | | |
|---|---|---|---|
| *Gains on business assets* | | *Gains on non-business assets\** | |
| *Number of complete years after 5 April 1998 for which asset held* | *Percentage of gain chargeable* | *Number of complete years after 5 April 1998 for which asset held* | *Percentage of gain chargeable* |
| 0 | 100 | 0 | 100 |
| 1 | 50 | 1 | 100 |
| 2 | 25 | 2 | 100 |
| 3 | 25 | 3 | 95 |
| 4 | 25 | 4 | 90 |
| 5 | 25 | 5 | 85 |
| 6 | 25 | 6 | 80 |
| 7 | 25 | 7 | 75 |
| 8 | 25 | 8 | 70 |
| 9 | 25 | 9 | 65 |
| 10 or more | 25 | 10 or more | 60 |
| \*Add one extra year if owned on 17 March 1998. | | | |

value as at 31 March 1982 whichever gives the smaller gain or loss in each case. Alternatively, you can elect to adopt the 31 March value for all of your assets held before that date. Such an election, once made and notified to the tax inspector, cannot be changed.

## How to calculate a capital gain or loss

To calculate any capital gains or losses prior to 6 April 2008, you need to prepare a schedule showing a brief description of all the non-exempted assets you have sold; the date and cost of acquisition; value at 31 March 1982 if held at that date; the date of disposal and disposal proceeds.

The next step is to calculate the 'unindexed gain or loss' but at this stage you must decide the figure of cost you are going to adopt (see table above). You can then work out the gain or loss.

If the result is an unindexed loss, this will be the figure you enter in the tax return; if an unindexed gain arises, then refer to the paragraphs on inflation on page 137.

**As from 6 April 2008, indexation and tapering relief as described above, has been abolished and there is now no relief for inflation when calculating any capital gains or losses.**

## Paying capital gains tax

Capital gains tax is payable, with any balance of income tax due, on the following 31 January each year. If you sell an asset on which you have a capital gain on the 6 April rather than on 5 April you will have an extra year before having to pay the capital gains tax.

Capital gains tax can be deferred by subscribing for new shares through the enterprise investment scheme (EIS) or new shares in approved quoted venture capital trusts (VCT); in such cases the capital gains tax deferral is in addition to the 20 per cent income tax relief (see page 163).

## Business assets

The capital gains legislation has always been very complicated and there has always been special categories of business that have had their only exemptions, rules and regulations. It is important to seek professional advice, particularly in dealing with business assets.

Following the abolition of indexation relief and the restructuring of the capital gains tax rates, an entrepreneurs relief is being introduced from 6 April 2008 whereby the first £1 million of gains from the sale of a trading business will be charged to capital gains tax at 10 per cent. Gains in excess of £1 million will be charged at 18 per cent.

## Roll-over relief

This relief allows you to defer the capital gains tax bill when you sell or dispose of assets in your business, providing you replace them within three years after the sale (or the 12 months prior to the sale). The whole of the sale proceeds must be so re-invested to defer the entire gain.

You can make a claim for roll-over relief within five years from 31 January following the end of the relevant tax year.

## What to enter in your 2008 tax return

Refer to page 53 where the *Capital gains* supplementary pages are reproduced.

Remembering that the 2008 tax return will apply to capital gains for the year ending 5 April 2008, if your total proceeds of sale do not exceed £36,800 and/or your chargeable gains do not exceed £9,200, there is no need to make any entry at all in this part of your tax return unless you are claiming allowable losses or wish to make some other claim or election. However, it is wise to keep all your schedules and workings.

As already mentioned, the capital gains tax legislation is very complicated – only a brief outline has been given here. There are, for example, complex rules for valuing assets held before the introduction of this tax in 1965; there are 'pooling' provisions for identical shares acquired on different dates; there are special rules for business assets and connected persons.

## Inherited assets (chargeable assets acquired)

Contrary to many people's belief, you do not generally have to pay capital gains tax on receiving cash or assets left to you under a will or settlement. Assets only become liable (subject to the normal exemption rules) when you dispose of them. The probate value will be used as the base cost of these assets.

## Selling or letting your house

Any profit you make on selling the property you own and live in is free from capital gains tax. Where you own two houses at the same time as a result of not being able to sell the first, no capital gains will arise on either house provided you sell the first house within three years. See page 154 for divorced persons.

Many people worry that if they let part of their home, then they will have to pay capital gains tax on part of the profits they make when it is sold. In fact, you can claim letting relief to reduce any capital gains liability.

You do this by working out what proportion the let part of the property bears to the total and apply this to any capital profit. Against that profit you can claim capital gains tax letting relief of the lower of £40,000 or the apportioned gain before any capital gains tax liability is assessed.

The last three years of ownership of your home always counts as a period of residence, so if you move out and let the property during that time it will not affect your exemption.

If you use part of your house exclusively for business then, when you sell the house, you may be liable to capital gains tax on that proportion that was used for business purposes although business asset taper relief could apply (prior to 6 April 2008) and roll-over relief (see page 140). This is unlikely to apply if you are an employee working from home occasionally unless a material part of the house is in fact used exclusively for business.

Get professional advice if you plan to sell off part of your garden – there are complicated capital gains tax rules.

## Windfalls from building societies, etc.

It has been common practice over the last few years for mutual insurance companies to pay out 'windfall proceeds' to their members.

These are liable to capital gains tax if, when added to any other capital gains you have incurred, the total exceeds the annual exemption amount (see page 136). This area has become more complex of late with some schemes being designed by insurance companies to avoid their members paying capital gains tax, so do read any paperwork carefully, and contact the insurance company or your tax office if you are unclear.

## Seek professional advice

If your financial affairs are not too complicated, capital gains tax can be fairly straightforward. However, only a brief outline of the tax has been covered in this book, so do seek professional advice if you are in any way unclear about the taxable effects of selling or gifting assets.

For more background information the tax office issue a free leaflet, CGT/FS1, available from any tax office.

# CHAPTER 16

# Inheritance tax

Most of the chapters in this book have dealt with tax payable on your income. Chapter 15 dealt with tax payable on capital items (capital gains tax) when such assets change hands during your lifetime.

Having paid all such liabilities, you are still not free of the tax inspector, for inheritance tax may have to be considered. Inheritance tax may be payable not only on the value of your estate on death, but also on lifetime gifts.

Most taxes have complex rules and provisions, mainly to avoid fraud, and this tax is certainly no exception. In this book it is only possible to deal broadly with the main provisions and exemptions. You should consult an accountant or solicitor if you need specific planning advice, or if you have to deal with someone else's estate.

It used to be assumed that this tax was only paid by those who had lots of money and assets, but the exemption limit for inheritance tax for 2007–2008 was only £300,000. With the appreciation in value of private house prices in particular over the last ten or 20 years, plus any savings, investments and other assets you may have and maybe proceeds from life assurance and pension fund lump sums, more and more people are beginning to realise that this tax is in fact applicable to them, and when they die, their estate will have to pay a large tax bill unless they do something about it now and consider some inheritance planning measures.

## Exemption limits and rates of tax

On deaths arising after 5 April 2008, an estate is liable to pay inheritance tax at a flat rate of 40 per cent on the value of the net assets in excess of £312,000. This exemption level is to increase to £325,000 for 2009–2010 and £350,000 for 2010–2011.

It was announced on 9 October 2007, and confirmed in the budget, that any unused exemption amount on a first death of a partner to a marriage or civil partnership can be added to a remaining partner's exemption limit. In other words, on the death of the first partner if say 50 per cent of the exemption amount at the time of death was unused then that percentage could be added to the exemption amount available to the remaining partner.

The estate of someone who dies on active service is exempt from inheritance tax.

## What is the value of your estate for inheritance purposes?

You need to identify six sets of figures as follows:

* List all your assets at their current value;

* Deduct any outstanding liabilities (mortgages, loans etc.);

* Add any likely life assurance receipt (although you can avoid this – see page 147);

* Deduct any tax free legacies stated in your will (see below);

* Add any potentially exempt gifts you have made in the previous seven years after allowing for any tax free gifts (see page 145);

* Add any gifts with reservation (see page 145);

The total of this calculation is now the net value of your estate for inheritance tax purposes.

Note that an additional tax charge may be payable during your lifetime on certain chargeable lifetime transfers and pre-owned assets (see page 146).

Remember that all assets passing between married couples and civil partners either by bequest under a will or under the rules governing the estate of anyone dying intestate (that is someone who has not made a will) are free of inheritance tax regardless of the total value.

HMRC have a leaflet (IHT 15) *Inheritance tax; how to calculate the liability*, available free from tax offices or their website.

The following paragraphs give more detail about the various gifts and transfers that might arise when considering this incredibly complicated tax.

## Tax-free legacies on death

The following legacies are allowed as a deduction from your estate for inheritance tax purposes:

* Legacies made for the benefit of the nation or for the public benefit, including funds to maintain historic property.

* Legacies made between husband and wife and civil partners, provided both are domiciled in the UK.

* Legacies to a charity.

* Legacies to political parties.

- Legacies of certain heritage property and woodlands.

## Lifetime gifts

Gifts fall into three categories as far as the inheritance tax rules are concerned: some gifts are specifically tax free and can be ignored; other gifts are exempt provided they were not made within seven years of death; and the third category covers chargeable lifetime transfers and gifts with reservations.

## Tax-free gifts

The following are gifts which are exempt:

1. All gifts between a husband and wife and between civil partners, if both are domiciled in the UK (if not, the limit is £55,000).

2. Gifts up to a total of £3,000 in any one year plus any unused amount of the previous year's exemption. (You can carry over unused relief for a maximum of one year.)

3. In addition to the £3,000 referred to above, individual gifts not exceeding £250 each to different persons in any one tax year (to an unlimited number of people as long as they don't form part of a larger gift).

4. Additional gifts if a person makes them as part of normal habitual expenditure made out of income.

5. Gifts arranged beforehand in consideration of marriage or civil partnership as follows:

| | Maximum gift limit £ |
|---|---|
| Between each partner | 2,500 |
| Parents of either | 5,000 each |
| Grandparents or more remote relatives of either | 2,500 |
| Any other person | 1,000 |

(The gifts must be made before the actual wedding day.)

6. All gifts to political parties, or UK-established charities.

7. Lump sums received from a pension scheme on death or retirement if used to purchase a pension for yourself or dependants.

8. Gifts for the benefit of the nation or public (for example, universities, the National Trust).

9. Maintenance payments to ex-husbands, ex-wives or ex-civil partners.

10. Reasonable gifts to support a dependant relative.

11. Gifts for the education and maintenance of your children, if under 18.

## All other gifts within seven years of death

These are known as potentially exempt transfers (PETs) and are tax free once you have lived for seven years from making the gift. If you die before the end of the seven-year period, the value of the gift is added to your estate for inheritance tax purposes, although there is a reduction in the *tax payable* on the gift on a tapering scale as follows:

| Years between gift and death | 0–3 | 3–4 | 4–5 | 5–6 | 6–7 |
|---|---|---|---|---|---|
| Percentage of inheritance tax payable | 100 | 80 | 60 | 40 | 20 |

## Gifts with reservation

These are gifts you have made but you continue to use yourself, for example, gifting your house but continuing to live in it yourself without paying a market rent – this would become a chargeable gift.

## Chargeable lifetime transfers and pre-owned assets

Prior to April 2006, it was quite common for individuals to avoid (or reduce) any future inheritance tax liability by setting up various forms of trust. However, since that date new legislation has been enacted that substantially reduces these benefits or creates another tax charge.

To close down or restructure existing trusts, or set up new ones, it is vital that you get professional advice for the tax legislation is a minefield.

Similarly some individuals made arrangements to reduce their inheritance tax liability by gifting or selling an asset at below its full market value by way of a trust or whatever but who continued to benefit from that asset.

Since 6 April 2005 any such benefit can attract a tax charge.

The taxable benefit is calculated on the market rent value in the case of land or property and in the case of other assets the benefit will be considered to be 6.25 per cent per year of its market value. No tax charge will arise where the benefit is less than £5,000 per year and it does not apply to assets you ceased to own prior to 18 March 1986.

Details of any benefit arising has to be declared in your main tax return, boxes 18 and 19.

The legislation is complicated and you almost certainly need to seek professional advice, for there are a number of exclusions and transitional reliefs.

There is a website for further information on **www.hmrc.gov.uk/ poa** – also ask your tax office for leaflets IHT 500 and IHT 501 by telephoning 0845 234 1000.

## Who pays the inheritance tax bill?

It is the responsibility of the executors of a will to pay any taxes due within six months from the date of death before distributing the assets to the beneficiaries. However, in the case of gifts made within the seven-year rule, executors could ask the person receiving the gift to pay the tax relating to the value of that gift, unless there is a clause in the will specifically authorising the estate to be responsible for paying any tax due, or the estate has insufficient funds to pay any tax liability.

It is important to remember that any inheritance tax has to be paid before assets can be distributed, and to emphasise the fact that all the assets are therefore frozen until the tax liability is agreed and settled.

## Quick-succession relief

If a second death in a family occurs within five years of the first death the second tax bill is reduced by the ratio that the value of the estate on the first death bears to the value at the second death, to which needs to be added any inheritance tax paid on that first death. For example, assume the value of the estate at the first death was £400,000, on which inheritance tax was paid, and the estate value at the second death was £500,000, then the inheritance tax bill on the estate of the second death would be reduced by the ratio 5:4.

Under quick-succession relief, if there was more than one year between the deaths, the calculation is reduced by 20 per cent for each full year.

## Small businesses and agricultural concerns

Over the past few years, most budgets have extended reliefs to reduce the impact of inheritance tax on the transfer of interests in small businesses and agricultural concerns. There are now substantial inheritance tax concessions – often reducing the liability to zero – if you own such a business concern.

The rules, regulations and conditions, on the type of business and period of ownership prior to death, are numerous and complex. It is important to consult professional advisers when considering such matters.

## Unmarried partners

Under the tax legislation, married couples and same-sex couples who are registered as civil partners are now treated equally for all tax legislation. However, heterosexual couples who live together do not get the same rights – they are treated as single persons for all tax legislation (but not for all social security legislation) so it is particularly important that each couple gives serious thought to the question of making a will and what happens to the home and property when one partner dies.

## Ways to reduce inheritance tax exposure

Most tax schemes to reduce inheritance tax are inevitably aimed at married couples or those who have entered into civil partnerships.

The following ideas should be considered and discussed with your solicitor or an independent financial adviser who specialises in inheritance tax. Such professionals should ideally be members of the Society of Trust and Estate Practitioners (STEP). The society can be contacted for a list of members in your area on 020 7838 4885 or their website **www.step.org**.

1. Make a will in order to make it clear to whom you wish your assets to pass on your death and to specify any personal wishes, gifts to family, friends, charities, etc., otherwise you will die intestate and cause unnecessary stress and problems for your family and dependants (see below).

2. Consider holding savings, investments and other assets in joint names to spread the ownership to reduce individual estate valuations.

3. Prior to the changes announced in the pre-budget report in October 2007 (see page 142) it was thought prudent for married couples or civil partners to hold the deeds of their main residence as tenants in common, not as joint tenants, so that each partner's share (and it does not have to be in equal parts) is independent of the other and can be sold or given away as that party wishes so that when one partner dies only 50 per cent (or the agreed share) will be valued in their estate. Now that it is possible to transfer any unused inheritance tax exemption limit, this is not so necessary.

4. Giving assets away in your lifetime obviously has the likelihood of reducing any inheritance tax liability, but bear in mind there may be capital gains to consider.

5. Life assurance should be considered, particularly for young to middle-aged partners, but do ensure the policy is written in trust

otherwise any lump sum paid out on death will be added to your estate, thus increasing the probability of a higher inheritance tax liability.

6. Certain investments, if held for a certain length of time, are exempt from inheritance tax. These include investments in woodlands, agricultural property or shares quoted on the alternative investment market (AIM) and enterprise investment schemes.

7. As a last resort, if you are left property under a will, and you either do not want it or you wish to pass it on to someone else (perhaps to avoid future tax liabilities), then you can effect a deed of variation within two years of the date of death.

8. Always bear in mind that a settlor cannot also be a beneficiary – and you must relinqish all title and control over an asset if it is to escape the clutches of the inheritance tax net.

## Wills

You should always make a will regardless of how much you own. This will prevent your dependants being unduly troubled and will mean that your wishes will be carried out legally and properly. Although there are do-it-yourself will packages available, it does not cost a lot to go through a solicitor, and you will then have expert, experienced advice on which to draw.

If you don't leave a valid will, you will be regarded as having died intestate and your assets will be distributed under strict legal rules, which may not be what you intended.

Many people make reference to specific charities in their will, stating to whom they would like to make legacies. The only problem with this is that if you wish to change the charities you have selected, you have to make a new will. You can get over this by leaving the legacies to the Charities Aid Foundation, giving them a list of the charities you wish to benefit. You can then change this list at any time, thus saving you the legal costs of changing your will.

The various law societies have lists of solicitors who specialise in wills and probate. In England and Wales the helpline is 020 7242 1222, in Scotland 0131 226 7411 and in Northern Ireland 028 9023 1614.

## Pension schemes

If you have a pension scheme, you are approaching 75 and you have not yet organised an annuity, check with your pension adviser or solicitor to ensure the fund is not going to be liable to inheritance tax.

# CHAPTER 17

# Family tax matters

Whether you are starting your first job, getting married, saving money, working on your own or retiring, you cannot escape the tax inspector.

Many people experience great difficulty in commucating with their tax office for one reason or another, particularly in claiming tax repayments. The secret behind dealing with any tax matter is to comply with the system. The whole of our tax system revolves around filling in forms at the right time (see Chapter 3 on page 16).

Either telephone your tax office, or call in or write and ask for the correct form, depending upon your circumstances. Fill it in and send it to your tax office in order to start the ball rolling. Always state your tax reference number. These days many of the forms are also available on the website, **www.hmrc.gov.uk**, so you can download them from there.

If you are taxed under PAYE, write to the tax office that deals with your employer's PAYE. If you are self-employed you will deal with the inspector who covers your business address.

Here are some practical steps to bear in mind.

## Starting work
### PAYE
You will need a tax code number (see page 98).

Your employer will fill in a form P45 and give this to you. You then select which of the statements A, B or C applies to you, and complete the rest of the form.

If, however, you decide to work for yourself, or in partnership with someone else, you will eventually have to fill in a tax return on which you will claim your allowances and declare your income. Thus the PAYE system will not apply to you and all you need to do is to tell your tax office when your business commences (see page 118).

### National insurance contributions
National insurance contributions are levied at varying rates depending on how much you earn, whether you are contracted out and whether you are an employee or self-employed. See Chapter 14 on page 130 for further details.

## Changes in allowances and deductions

Most tax allowances and tax credits are not given to you automatically – they have to be claimed and the claim must be supported by the right information.

The more common instances of changes in allowances and credits are covered in this chapter.

## Married couples and same-sex couples

Same-sex partners who registered their relationship in a civil partnership on or after 5 December 2005 are entitled to the same income tax, inheritance tax and pension and tax credits as married couples. What should such partners do to benefit fully from the tax system?

1. **Personal allowances.** Both partners get a personal allowance in their own right; it will be wasted if neither work and have no income at all – it cannot be transferred from one to the other.

   To avoid one partner losing the personal allowance, consider transferring investments or savings so that the income can be offset against the other partner's personal allowance.

2. **Married couple's allowance.** If one partner was born before 6 April 1935, then you can claim married couple's allowance. Refer to page 93 to see if it is beneficial to transfer this allowance.

3. **Higher rate tax.** If a husband or wife or partner is paying tax at the higher rate (40 per cent), then transferring some income-producing assets between them would be beneficial if one partner is on the basic rate tax band or is not using all of their personal allowance.

   Sometimes a partner may be reluctant to transfer cash or assets in case they may be 'spent'. One solution is to transfer certain assets into joint ownership as 'tenants in common'. Whilst the original owner could retain, say, a 95 per cent share, the tax office would treat the income as being split 50:50 if no declaration of actual ownership is made. In some cases it may be beneficial to make a declaration of ownership, in which case ask the tax office for form 17 before the start of a tax year (you cannot backdate such a request).

4. **Age-related allowances.** Partners aged 65 and over should similarly check that their tax affairs are organised as above because both the higher personal allowance, which each of them gets in their own right, and the married couple's allowance, if applicable, are reduced if their incomes exceed certain limits (see page 111).

5. **Covenants.** Ensure that tax relief on covenants is not lost (see page 89).

6. **Capital gains.** If at all practicable, ensure that your investments are allocated between you or held in joint names so that you can each take full benefit of the capital gains exemption limit when investments are sold.

7. **Stakeholder pensions.** Each partner can pay up to £3,600 a year into a pension fund even if you have no earnings. Consider setting up pension funds for a non-working husband or wife or civil partner and/or children. These pensions are dealt with in more detail on page 164.

## Raising a family

As soon as your baby is born, ask at your local benefits agency office for a child benefit claim form. Complete this and return it to them with the birth certificate.

Child benefit is normally payable to the mother and paid direct into her bank account each month (see page 185). The benefit is tax free.

Apply also for the child tax credit by telephoning 0845 300 3900 (see page 93).

## Child trust funds

Since 1 September 2002 you have been entitled to receive a voucher from the Government for £250 when you have a baby and you can claim double this amount if you are entitled to the full child tax credit (see page 93) if your household income is at or below the child tax credit income threshold. A further £250 (or £500) will be paid when the child reaches the age of seven but these payments will not start until 2009. You must pay these vouchers into a bank or building society trust fund of your choice; there are several options to choose from nowadays.

Banks, building societies, etc. offer child trust fund accounts – either deposit accounts where there will be little risk with modest growth; stakeholder funds where there will be some exposure to stockmarket fluctuations but where the charges must not exceed 1.5 per cent; or non-stakeholder funds where there will be a higher risk, probably higher growth but no cap on charges.

If you do not open an appropriate account within 12 months of the voucher being issued, then the Government will open a stakeholder account for you.

At no stage until the child's 18th birthday can there be any withdrawals, but you can move the account from one provider to another. Income earned from the fund will be free of income tax and capital gains tax.

Once the child reaches the age of 18 then he or she can use the money for any purpose whatsoever.

Additional funds can be invested in the trust account by parents or indeed anyone else (they do not have to be related to the child) up to an extra £1,200 a year, with a minimum contribution of £10. A fact sheet is available on the internet on **www.childtrustfund.gov.uk** or call the trust helpline on 0845 302 1470.

For funds maturing on or after 2020, you can roll over the investment or deposit into an ISA (see page 160).

## Childcare facilities

Employees can benefit from the use of childcare facilities provided by and paid for directly by their employer without incurring a tax or national insurance charge on that benefit.

To qualify for the exemption:

1. The child must be under 18.

2. The premises must not be domestic premises.

3. The premises must be provided by the employer (or a group of employers or a local authority) with each employer(s) being responsible for finance and management.

## Childcare voucher scheme

Employers can set aside up to £55 per week out of an employee's salary as a contribution towards the cost of registered childcare, including nurseries, nannies, crèches and after-school clubs, for under 16 year olds – in other words this is a specific salary sacrifice by the employee and it is free of income tax and national insurance. Each parent's employer can be involved in such a scheme, effectively giving a total of £110 per week as a maximum.

This scheme is not available for the self-employed.

There is a useful website reference address you can visit on **www.daycaretrust.org.uk**.

## Children's income

Each child is an individual taxpayer entitled to his or her own personal allowance. Parents are not taxable on a child's casual earnings nor on income arising on gifts from relatives. However, if you give cash or property to your children other than through the child trust fund scheme, the income will be treated as yours for income tax purposes if it exceeds £100 gross in the year.

In spite of the above, even if parents did give each of their children say £1,400 (outside the child trust fund), then at say 6 per cent this would still be under the 'taxable limit' and the interest would be tax free.

The only way in which parents could transfer larger sums to their children without continuing to pay tax on the income from those assets was by setting up an irrecoverable trust, which could accumulate income until the child was 18. However, if income was paid direct to the child before then, it was taxed as the income of the parent. You should consult a professional adviser regarding the current taxation legislation of trusts.

On the other hand, a child can receive, or benefit from, income provided by a relative, either by the gift of investments or by setting up a trust that pays out income for the child's education and maintenance.

In these cases you should ask your tax office for form 232 on which to declare your child's income and, if the income has had tax deducted before receipt, for example trust income, interest, etc., claim a tax repayment in respect of the child's personal allowance.

## Students

Earnings from holiday jobs will often have PAYE tax deducted. Ask your employer for form P38(S) which, when completed and returned, will enable payment to be made without tax deductions if the student does not earn above the personal allowance of £5,435 for 2008–2009 (£5,225 for 2007–2008).

Student loan repayments to a new borrower are collected under the PAYE system once employment commences, and the employer has to deduct repayments depending on the income level. These 'income contingent student loans' as they are called, have to be acknowledged in your tax return (see page 24).

If you change jobs frequently, your loan account could be incorrect, so it is important to check your annual statement regularly. You can also ring the helpline 0870 240 6298.

## One-parent families

In addition to the personal allowance, you should consider claiming the various tax credits as detailed in Chapter 9 on page 92.

## Divorce or separation

Inform the tax office of your changed circumstances. Obviously both parties keep their personal tax allowances and if you have been claiming married couple's allowance, then this will continue until the end of the tax year in which separation took place.

Any claim for child tax credit may have to be reassessed depending on which partner looks after the children – or, indeed, apportioned if a child is to spend some time living with each partner (see page 93).

In the case of a woman who is paying national insurance contributions at the reduced rate, then you should reconsider your position to see if you need to pay full-rate contributions to protect your benefits. (Ask for leaflet CA10, *National Insurance contributions for divorced women*, available from your tax office.)

See page 88 for maintenance payments and page 167 for pension rights.

As regards the family home, if one partner sells, or gives it to the other within three years of the separation, there will be no capital gains tax payable; and still no tax will be payable if, after that period, one of the partners still resides there and the other partner has not claimed any other property as a main home.

## Death of a wife or husband or civil partner

On death, any married couple's allowance or blind person's allowance still unused is transferred to the surviving partner for the remainder of that tax year; similarly any unused inheritance tax exemption will be transferred to a remaining partner.

A tax-free bereavement payment can also be claimed from the Department for Work and Pensions (DWP) by either a widow, a widower or surviving civil partner, subject to certain conditions.

See Chapter 16 on page 12 regarding any inheritance tax liabilities.

Additionally, bereavement allowance and widowed parent's allowance might be available from the DWP, depending on your national insurance status and contributions.

## Ceasing employment

### Permanently

Send parts 2 and 3 of form P45, which your employer will have given you, to your tax office; the district is shown on the form. Also write a letter confirming that you have either retired, ceased working or have become self-employed, and claim any tax repayment.

### Temporarily

When you change employment or are made redundant and there is a gap between one job and the next, you will need to hand in form P45 when you sign on to claim benefits. The Jobcentre Plus will advise you on the proportion of your jobseeker's allowance that is taxable and will deal with any tax refund due at the end of the tax year. Alternatively, if you are not entitled to benefits, send in your P45 to your tax office telling them you are temporarily unemployed. This may result in a tax refund.

If you do not start a new job by the following 5 April, check your total income and tax, as shown in Chapter 11 (page 100), to see if there is a repayment or underpayment of tax due, and if you have been claiming jobseeker's allowance or income support and you return to work then complete form ES40 and the Jobcentre will send you a P45 form for you to take to your new employer.

## Making a will

It is important to make a will. See page 148 for more details.

## Are you claiming your tax refund?

There are broadly two main categories of people who should consider claiming tax refunds.

### Savers with building society and bank accounts

Interest paid by building societies and banks will have had tax deducted from it at the savings rate (20 per cent) before it is paid to you.

If your total income is less than your personal allowance – as will often be the case for children, husbands or wives or civil partners who are not earning or are on low incomes – then you should claim that tax back.

Ask your bank or building society for form R85, fill it in and return it to them. Once they have this form, they can pay you interest in future without first deducting tax.

Even if your total income does exceed your personal allowance, the savings rate of tax is only 10 per cent so you can claim the difference between the two rates on the first £2,320 of savings income (£2,230 for 2007–2008), although if your non-savings income is above this limit the 10 per cent rate will not be applicable.

## Pensioners

The above comments also apply to pensioners but, in addition, many pensioners whose income is less than their age-related allowance may also be receiving additional pensions and other interest on which tax has been deducted. Again, many will be entitled to tax refunds (see Chapter 12 on page 108).

## To claim a tax refund

Write to any tax office asking for leaflet IR110. This gives you some helpful information and, in particular, the leaflet contains a form for you to fill in and return to your tax office requesting a tax refund (see page 105 for further details).

## Living abroad

If you retire abroad, you will still be liable to UK tax on any income you receive from the UK over and above your UK tax allowances; any income you receive abroad will be taxed according to that country's tax regulations. Some countries have a double taxation agreement with the UK, in which case you may get taxed under local tax regulations and not those of the UK. See page 56 as regards non-residency and period of visits to the UK.

You will also need to familiarise yourself with local legislation as regards inheritance tax and local forms of death duties.

As regards your social security, healthcare and pension rights, if you live in the European Community, contact the DSS overseas branch at Tyneview Park, Newcastle upon Tyne, NE98 1YX, who publish a free leaflet on these matters and can advise you on your personal situation.

# CHAPTER 18

# Money matters

As well as taking care of your family tax affairs, it is a good idea to know some of the best kinds of financial planning available, not only for the present but also for the future.

Refer to Chapter 17 on page 149 to ensure that you have allocated investments between partners to make the best use of the tax system.

## Savings and investment opportunities

There are five important issues to consider when deciding where to invest your savings. Make sure that:

- You have some savings where you can get at your money quickly in an emergency.

- You are making full use of tax-free savings.

- You are not putting money into taxable investments where you are unable to reclaim, or offset, any tax deducted.

- You are not limiting social security benefits by getting income from investments.

- You are not taking unnecessary risks or, at least if you are, do ensure that you understand the full repercussions if things go wrong.

Various savings opportunities and their tax implications are now considered below.

## Building society deposit or share accounts

These combine safety with easy access and a flexible rate of interest. They are particularly useful if you are saving for eventual house purchase as building societies tend to give preference to existing investors.

Interest is paid after having the tax deducted at the rate of 20 per cent. If your total income is unlikely to exceed your personal allowance you can fill in form R85, and once the building society receive this completed form they will pay interest gross (see page 114).

Note, however, that cash windfalls on a building society takeover/conversion may be liable to capital gains tax and a cash windfall on a merger may be liable to income tax (see page 141).

## Bank deposit accounts

Banks are now more flexible in the variety of deposit accounts and interest you can have to suit your particular needs. The interest has tax deducted at the rate of 20 per cent, but non-taxpayers can receive payments gross by filling in the appropriate form (see building society accounts above).

## Offshore accounts

Many people invest in offshore building society or bank accounts in order to benefit from receiving interest gross and paying tax later. Such cash flow advantage can be lost, however, if you have to make tax payments on account during the year under self assessment. Also, there could be repayment delays and local probate problems in the event of death.

The interest must be declared on your tax return and, under the European Savings Directive which came into force on 1 July 2005, banks within the EU and certain other countries are required to report details of the income you receive from overseas accounts to the tax office. You either have to agree to let the bank tell the tax authorities about the interest or suffer a 15 per cent witholding tax.

In addition, certain countries or territories which were reluctant to comply with the information-exchange requirements of the directive have opted instead to withold tax on interest payments; these countries include Jersey, Guernsey and the Isle of Man.

## National Savings accounts

Like a building society account, this is an easy method of saving and money is easily withdrawn. Only the first £70 of interest in the National Savings ordinary account is tax free. The investment and ordinary account interest is paid gross but is still taxable and should be shown in your tax return.

The National Savings ordinary accounts are now closed for transactions and have been replaced by easy access savings accounts; savers with existing ordinary accounts should have received a letter from National Savings and Investments suggesting they transfer their account into this new type of account. The easy access savings account pays a higher rate of interest, which will still be paid gross, and there will be more flexibility. National Savings and Investments have a helpline on 0845 366 6667. There is also a general advice line on 0845 964 5000 and a website **www.nsandi.com**.

## National Savings certificates

There are two types of certificate: fixed interest and index linked. With both types, interest is added to your capital and paid at the end of the fixed period (there are varying periods for which you can purchase these certificates). Interest is free of income tax and capital gains tax and you do not have to declare it on your tax return. If you do have to cash in a certificate before the expiry date, you will lose part of your interest but your capital will be secure.

## National Savings income bonds

These are designed for savers who wish to receive regular monthly payments of interest whilst at the same time preserving the full cash value of their investment. The variable interest is paid monthly without tax being deducted. However, the interest is taxable and should be declared in your tax return. There are also available fixed rate savings bonds if you want to know that the rate of interest is guaranteed at a certain level rather than variable.

## Pensioners guaranteed income bonds

These bonds are no longer on sale but this will not affect current holders. The bonds will remain valid until they mature.

These National Savings bonds carry a fixed rate of interest for five years but you could also consider one-year and two-year bonds. They were specifically for people over 60 years of age.

The gross interest is paid monthly and should be declared in your tax return.

Consider as an alternative guaranteed income bonds.

## National Savings capital bonds

These bonds are no longer on sale but you can continue with any existing holdings until they mature. These are similar to income bonds except that a guaranteed rate of interest is added to the five-year bond each year. The amount of interest is added gross, but you do have to declare the interest in your tax return every year and pay tax on it (if you are a taxpayer), even though you have not actually received the interest.

Consider as an alternative guaranteed growth bonds.

## National Savings guaranteed equity bonds

These are five-year investments with the return linked to the FTSE 100 index; however, if the index has fallen by the end of the five-year period the intial investment will be paid in full. Any interest earned is added at maturity and is liable to tax and any capital gain will be subject to capital gains tax.

### Children's bonus bonds
A high-interest savings scheme for children under the age of 16. The bonds can be purchased at any post office. Interest is added on each anniversary plus a bonus on the fifth anniversary (up to the age of 21). Both the interest and bonus is tax free and parents can fund these without affecting their own tax liability.

### Tax-exempt special savings account (TESSA)
TESSAs were replaced with the new tax-free individual savings account (ISA) from 6 April 1999.

### TOISA accounts
When your TESSA matures you could transfer the capital into a TESSA-only ISA (TOISA) account within six months of maturity and this will not count towards the usual ISA limits (see below) so you can still use the maximum annual ISA investment of £7,200 for 2008–2009.

### Personal equity plans (PEPs)
The tax benefits of a PEP were that any dividends received and any re-invested interest would be free from tax, and any capital gains would be free of capital gains tax.

All-employee share schemes could also be transferred to a single-company PEP without incurring capital gains tax.

PEPs have now been replaced with the new tax-free individual savings account (ISA) but existing PEPs continue and you can still transfer to another PEP provider, but do check the charges carefully before you transfer.

### Individual savings account (ISA)
All income and capital gains arising from these accounts is free of tax and does not have to be shown in your tax return.

All UK residents over the age of 16 can open such accounts regardless of the value of any existing PEPs or TOISAs. Husbands and wives and civil partners each have their own annual limits.

Prior to 6 April 2008 there were two types of ISA – maxi and mini. Under a maxi ISA, savers could spread their money between cash deposits, shares and insurance in a single plan run by one financial company. You could invest up to £7,000 a year, either all in stocks and shares, or up to £3,000 in cash (for example, National Savings, bank deposits) and the balance in shares.

With a mini ISA, savers could use one financial service provider for shares and another for cash (the life assurance option was withdrawn in April 2005). The maximum that could be invested in a mini ISA is again £7,000, but with a maximum holding in stocks and shares of £4,000.

From 6 April 2008 the distinction between maxi and mini ISAs is being abolished. The maximum annual investment limit is increased to £7,200 with the maximum cash component being £3,600.

## Friendly societies
You can invest up to £270 a year if paid in a lump sum, or £300 a year if paid monthly in a tax-exempt savings plan regardless of your age.

## Unit trusts
These are a way for the small investor to benefit from investing in a wide range of companies. Many trusts nowadays specialise in different areas of investment – some with emphasis on capital growth, or income, or overseas companies, etc. You can purchase units directly from the unit trust company, or through a bank or broker. You pay tax on the income and gains in the normal way.

## Purchased life annuities
These are covered in the Pensioners chapter on page 115.

## Endowment policies
Many people took out this form of insurance policy, often to 'cover' a possible contingency like paying off a mortgage or celebrating early retirement, but often the policy was not cashed in but continues to exist after its original purpose has perhaps become obsolete.

There is a sound financial market now for selling on these policies and you should get quotations from a professional advisor – contact the Association of Policy Market Makers 0845 833 0086, **www.apmm.org**. Financially it is usually best to hold onto a policy until maturity, especially if you are getting tax relief, which is available only to pre-14 March 1984 policies.

## Finance houses
These are businesses which generally pay a higher rate of interest than the average market rate. It is important to consult an accountant or solicitor to obtain an opinion as to a particular finance house's financial stability.

### Permanent interest-bearing shares (PIBs)

These are building society shares which are listed on the stock exchange and are traded on the stock market. There is a fixed rate of interest. They are not as secure as gilt-edged investments or building society accounts, and they are not as marketable when you wish to sell.

### Bonds

The bond market has expanded rapidly over the last few years with many variations such as investment bonds, guaranteed income bonds, fixed-rate bonds, etc. They are methods of investing lump sums. Watch carefully for hidden charges that could eat into your capital and bear in mind that you could lose if interest rates rise and you are locked into a fixed rate over a number of years. Tax is deducted from the interest when it is paid and cannot be reclaimed by non-taxpayers.

### Government stocks

These stocks, known as gilt-edged securities, are quoted on the stock exchange. They can be purchased through a bank or broker or through the Bank of England Registrar (telephone freephone 0800 818 614 for a form).

Interest is paid gross but if you do want to have tax deducted from your interest you can elect to do so when you buy the shares. Profits on sale are free from capital gains tax.

### Ordinary shares in quoted companies

Buying shares quoted on the stock exchange is a gamble, for the share price of even the most well-known names can fluctuate considerably over a short period. You should obtain professional advice before investing.

Dividends are paid after allowing for a tax credit.

If you are a non-taxpayer, this tax credit cannot be reclaimed and it may be more beneficial to put savings into investments that pay gross interest without any tax deductions.

The amount of dividend received, plus the tax credit, has to be added to your total income in working out your overall tax liability and if this takes you into the higher rate band, then more tax will be payable. If you are a basic rate taxpayer, there is no further liability.

## Enterprise investment scheme (EIS)

Under these schemes, an individual can gain tax relief on investments in unquoted trading companies. The main provisions are as follows:

1. Income tax relief is given at 20 per cent on qualifying investments up to £500,000 per year for 2008–2009 (£400,000 for 2007–2008).

2. Gains on disposal are exempt from capital gains tax.

3. There is income tax or capital gains tax relief for losses on disposal.

4. Eligible shares must be held for at least three years.

5. Relief on up to one half of the amount an individual invests between 6 April and 5 October in any year can be carried back to the previous tax year, subject to a maximum of £50,000 (£25,000 before April 2006).

6. A chargeable gain can be reinvested in an EIS to obtain a deferral of capital gains tax.

7. For eligible shares issued, the subscription has to be wholly in cash.

The rules and regulations governing these schemes are very complex. Do seek professional advice before investing.

## Venture capital trusts

These were introduced to encourage individuals to invest indirectly in unquoted trading companies.

The main provisions are:

1. Individuals are exempt from tax on dividends arising from shares acquired in these trusts, up to £200,000 a year.

2. Income tax relief of 30 per cent on up to £200,000 in any tax year for subscribing for new shares held for at least five years (three years for shares issued between 6 April 2000 and 5 April 2006).

3. For shares issued prior to 6 April 2004 capital gains tax deferred relief is available up to the annual investment limit.

There is useful reference material available from the British Venture Capital Association on 020 7025 2950, **www.bvca.co.uk**.

## Community investment relief
Investments made by individuals and companies on or after 17 April 2002 in a community development finance institution qualify for tax relief of 5 per cent a year of the investment for a period of five years.

## Investing in property
Investing in a second property may provide a safe investment over a longer period, even though any profit you might make on selling would be subject to capital gains tax. For tax relief on interest on borrowing for such a purpose, see page 87 and for the tax treatment of property income see page 84.

## Selling your house
Any profit you make on selling the property you own and live in is free from capital gains tax. See page 140 for the capital gains tax position where there is an overlap between buying and selling, and the situation regarding letting; also using your home for business.

## Charitable giving
There are many ways of giving to charity tax efficiently and these are all covered in Chapter 8 on page 87.

## Pension schemes
In general, contributing to a pension scheme is a good idea because:

1. You get tax relief at your top income tax rate.

2. The pension scheme will provide you with additional income to supplement your State pension when you retire.

3. A tax-free capital sum can be taken any time after retirement and under recent legislation, sometimes before retirement.

4. Employer's contributions to your scheme are not treated as a taxable benefit.

   However, there is no guarantee that pension funds will increase in value in the short term – they are essentially a long-term investment.

## How do you get tax relief on pension contributions?
1. If you are in an occupational pension scheme, your employer will deduct your contribution from your salary before PAYE tax is calculated – that way you will get relief at your highest tax rate.

2. If you are a member of a personal pension scheme or stakeholder scheme, basic rate tax is deducted when you pay the net premium;

if you are a higher rate taxpayer you claim the difference between this higher rate and the basic rate on your tax return.

3. For retirement annuity contracts (which were effectively personal pension plans taken out prior to 1 July 1998) you will pay the premium gross, and can claim tax relief in your tax return – although sometimes your PAYE tax code will have been adjusted to take the relief into account.

### Limits prior to 6 April 2006

Prior to 6 April 2006 the amount of tax-free cash you could claim on retirement, and the maximum pension and death benefits, were defined by a combination of tax legislation and the type of scheme.

The chart below identifies the maximum relevant earnings figures and the maximum allowable contribution limits for personal pension plans and retirement annuity contracts depending on your age at the beginning of the tax year.

| Maximum contribution limits prior to 6 April 2006 | | |
|---|---|---|
| Age at beginning of tax year | Retirement annuity premium percentage of income | Personal pension plan percentage of income |
| up to 35 | 17.5 | 17.5 |
| 36 to 45 | 17.5 | 20 |
| 46 to 50 | 17.5 | 25 |
| 51 to 55 | 20 | 30 |
| 56 to 60 | 22.5 | 35 |
| 61 and over | 27.5 | 40 |

*Note*
For plans taken out after 14 March 1989, the maximum net relevant earnings figures on which relief was available was as follows: £95,400 for 2001–2002, £97,200 for 2002–2003, £99,000 for 2003–2004, £102,000 for 2004–2005 and £105,600 for 2005–2006.

### Carrying back pension payments

This carry-back provision ceased to apply after the 2005–2006 tax year following the introduction of the new pension legislation.

### Current pension legislation

With effect from 6 April 2006, new pension legislation was introduced in order to make pensions easier to understand. The eight different and complex statutory pension rules and regulations that previously existed were swept away and replaced by one simplified, although not necessarily simpler, set of rules for all schemes.

The main provisions of the new pension legislation are as follows:

1. Subject to the rules of your pension scheme, there is no limit on the amount you can put into your pension pot and you can save in more than one type of pension scheme if you so wish.

2. You can get tax relief on contributions of up to 100 per cent of UK earnings if you are a UK taxpayer; if you are a non-taxpayer, every £100 of contributions will receive a contribution of £28 (£25 for 2008–2009) from the tax authorities up to a maximum of £3,600 per year.

3. There will be no carry-back or carry-forward arrangements.

4. There will be a maximum annual allowance for pension contributions (including any contributions from your employer) and if this is exceeded, there will be a tax charge of 40 per cent on the excess.

5. There will be a lifetime allowance on the total value of your pension schemes. If your pension savings exceed this you may be taxed on the excess at 25 per cent if you take additional savings as a pension and 55 per cent if you take them as a lump sum.

| Pension allowances | | |
|---|---|---|
| Tax year | Annual allowance £ | Lifetime allowance £ |
| 2006–2007 | 215,000 | 1,500,000 |
| 2007–2008 | 225,000 | 1,600,000 |
| 2008–2009 | 235,000 | 1,650,000 |
| 2009–2010 | 245,000 | 1,750,000 |
| 2010–2011 | 255,000 | 1,800,000 |

6. You will still get tax relief on your contributions as mentioned on page 164.

7. Your own scheme will define the earliest age at which you can retire, but by 6 April 2010 every pension scheme must have a minimum retirement age limit of at least 55.

8. You will be able to continue in employment after your official retirement age, even with the same employer, and you can take tax free cash of up to 25 per cent, subject to the rules of your pension scheme, even if you carry on working.

9. If the total value of your pension scheme is £15,000 or less and your scheme rules permit, then instead of taking a pension you may be able to take your entire fund as a lump sum; 25 per cent of

the fund would be tax free and the rest would be taxed as part of your income.

10. For the various options to consider on retirement see page 117.

There is a useful website at **www.hmrc.gov.uk/pensionschemes** and a helpline on 0115 974 1600.

### Other pension schemes
A self-invested personal pension (known as SIPPs) and small self-administered schemes (known as SSASs) are governed by the same pension rules detailed above, the main difference is that you have a wider range of investments to choose from rather than being restricted to those of an insurance company.

### Other pension issues
### Insolvency and pensions
Anyone filing for bankruptcy does not have to include any personal pension fund in their statement of assets, except where fraud could be established. Legislation already exists to protect money saved in occupational pension schemes from creditors and new legislation is currently being enacted which will give some protection to pension rights if an employer becomes insolvent.

### Part-timers and pension rights
Following recent legislation, anyone who has been prevented from joining an occupational pension scheme because of their part-time status can have pension rights backdated to 1976. Such employees must, however, still be working for the relevant company or lodge a claim within six months of leaving.

### Divorce and pension rights
The law allows for the allocation of pension funds and rights at the divorce date between husband and wife. However, this does not happen automatically and it needs to be discussed with your solicitor as part of the divorce settlement negotiations.

### If your pension provider goes out of business
The Pension Protection Fund and the Financial Assistance Scheme both exist to grant compensation to members of pension schemes that go out of business or whose members have lost out due to their scheme being underfunded and the employer becoming insolvent or where they no longer exist. Go to the following sites for information: **www.dwp.gov.uk** or **www.pensionprotectionfund.org.uk**.

## How to trace old pension schemes

Either contact your former employer or, failing that, contact the Pension Schemes Registry on 0191 225 6316. They also have a website at **www.thepensionsregulator.gov.uk**.

## Pension forecast

You can write to the Pension Service Retirement Pension Forecast Unit at Tyneview Park, Newcastle upon Tyne NE98 1BA to get a forecast of your likely State pension and SERPS entitlements.

There is also a telephone number 0845 300 0168 and a website at **www.thepensionservice.gov.uk**.

CHAPTER 19

# Calculating your own tax and the *Check Your Tax* calculator

If you want to calculate your tax when you send in your tax return, you need to ask for the tax calculation summary pages – telephone 0845 9000 404.

All the boxes are numbered according to the boxes in the main tax return and any supplementary pages that you need to complete, and although these forms look very complicated it is really a question of transferring all the figures into the correct summary boxes and following the instructions to ensure that you do the additions and subtractions according to the sequence. Because the tax office have to cover all possible tax situations, their working sheets are very comprehensive and lengthy.

You may find it more convenient to use the *Check Your Tax* calculator on the following pages; even if you don't want to do your own tax you may find the calculator useful to check the statements you get from the tax office.

Use the tax return working notes on pages 173–180 to jot down individual figures or use for calculations.

## *Check Your Tax* calculator

This layout is designed for the year ended 5 April 2008 but you could use it for earlier years provided you alter the tax rates and include the correct allowances (refer to page 187).

Do not include any income that is tax free (for example, PEPs, TESSAs, ISAs, the first £70 interest on National Savings ordinary accounts or National Savings certificate interest) – see pages 13–14.

---

### *Check Your Tax* calculator

| | Tax deducted | Gross amount |
|---|---|---|
| **Your non-savings income** | | |
| Salary or wages after deducting any pension scheme contribution or payroll giving | ................. | ................. |
| State pension | | ................. |
| Other pensions | ................. | ................. |
| Benefits from employer (see form P11D) | ................. | ................. |
| Profits from self-employment (usually the accounts period ending in the 2007–2008 tax year) or freelance earnings, after capital allowances and loss relief | | ................. |
| Casual earnings, after expenses | ................. | ................. |
| Social security benefits that are taxable | | ................. |
| Income from land and property, after expenses (exclude tax-free rental under rent-a-room scheme) | ................. | ................. |
| Total non-savings income | (a) £ ................. | (A) £ ................. |
| | | |
| **Less: Allowable expenses** | | |
| Personal pension contributions, including retirement annuity contribution for this year (exclude any contributions deducted from salary under PAYE above) | ................. | ................. |
| Market value of shares etc. and land and buildings gifted to charities | | ................. |
| Interest paid on qualifying loans | ................. | ................. |
| Other expenses allowed for tax | ................. | ................. |
| Total allowable expenses | (b) £ ................. | (B) £ ................. |
| | | |
| **Savings income (excluding dividends)** | | |
| Interest received | ................. | ................. |

---

|  | *Tax deducted* | *Gross amount* |
|---|---|---|
| **Dividend income** | | |
| Dividends received (you should add the tax credit to this and then show it separately in the tax-deducted column) | ................. | ................. |
| <u>Total savings and dividend income</u>   (c) £ ................. | | (C) £ ................. |
| <u>Total income and tax deducted</u>   a–b+c=(d) £ ................. | | (D) £ ................. |
| | | A-B+C=D |

**Less: Allowances claim**

| | | |
|---|---|---|
| Personal allowance/age allowance (but deduct any income limit reduction if over 65 – see table on page 187) | | ................. |
| Blind person's allowance | | ................. |
| <u>Income on which tax is payable</u> (D minus total allowances) | | (E) £ ................. |

**Tax payable**

(see band limits on page 187 and notes below)

| | | |
|---|---|---|
| **First** £2,230 of income at 10 per cent | | ................. |
| **Non-savings income** (see note 4) | | |
| £              at 22 per cent | | ................. |
| £              at 40 per cent | | ................. |
| **Savings income** | | |
| £              at 20 per cent | | ................. |
| £              at 40 per cent | | ................. |
| **Dividend income** | | |
| £              at 10 per cent | | ................. |
| £              at 32.5 per cent | | ................. |
| (E) £................. | Total (F) ................. | |

**Less:** Your claim for personal allowances
that are available at only 10 per cent

Married couple's allowance ................
(but note any restriction
– see page 92)

Maintenance or alimony
(max £2,440) ................

(G) £ ................@ 10 per cent = (H)£ ................

(F–H=I) £ ................

**Less:** Relief at the appropriate percentage for:
Enterprise investment scheme ................
Venture capital trust ................
Community investment ................

£ ................ = (J) £ ................

**Less:** Tax already deducted (d) £ ................

**Tax due** (or refundable if this is a minus figure) I – J – d = K   (K) £ ................

*Notes:*
1. You cannot reclaim the 10 per cent tax credit on dividends.
2. You will need to add to the tax due, any Class 4 national insurance liability, any capital gains tax liability and any underpayment from a previous year. (Deduct any tax repayment already received or any potential underpayment already in your tax code for a later year).
3. Your total tax liability will need to be adjusted for any carry back of gift aid.
4. The basic-rate band will be increased by the gross amount of the gift aid.

**Allocation of tax rate bands**
The sequence in which you calculate your tax rates is critical to the way the tax system works – refer to the sequence list on page 103.
You are taxed at 10 per cent of your first £2,230 of taxable income, whatever its source.
Then you pay 22 per cent on the next £32,370 of earned or pension income, or 20 per cent of savings income, and 10 per cent on dividend income.
After that, you pay 40 per cent on everything except dividend income, which is charged at 32.5 per cent.

# CHAPTER 20

# Tax return working notes

U se these boxes to make a note of how you compiled the figures that you put in your tax return or as a memory jogger.

---

**Interest and dividends received**

---

**Property income and expenses**

**Other income**

# Earnings and benefits

**Expenses claimed**

# Car details and car mileage notes

## Pension income and pension scheme notes

# Gift aid donations

**Capital gains notes**

**Inheritance tax notes**

# Useful reference numbers

## Taxation and national insurance

Child tax credit claim line: 0845 300 3900

Child tax credit helpline: 0845 300 3900

Construction industry helpline: 0845 733 5588

Construction industry order line: 0845 366 7899

HM Revenue and Customs main website: **www.hmrc.gov.uk**

HM Revenue and Customs pension scheme helpline: 0115 974 1600

HM Revenue and Customs pension scheme website
**www.hmrc.gov.uk/pensionschemes**

National insurance helpline for employees: 0191 225 7447

National insurance helpline for employers: 0845 714 3143

National insurance helpline for the self-employed: 0845 915 4655

Requests for tax forms and help sheets: 0845 900 0404

Short tax return helpline: 0845 302 1486

Taxback helpline: 0845 077 6543

Tax office helpline: 0845 900 0444

## Savings and pensions, etc.

Association of policy market makers (endowment policies) 0845 833
0086

British Venture Capital Association: 020 7025 2950, **www.bvca.co.uk**

Child trust fund help: 0845 302 1470, **www.childtrustfund.gov.uk**

Law societies for England and Wales: 020 7242 1222

Law societies for Northern Ireland: 0289 023 1614

Law societies for Scotland: 0131 226 7411

National Savings and Investments: 0845 964 5000, **www.nsandi.com**

Office of the pension advisory service: 0845 600 0806,
**www.opas.org.uk**

Pension schemes registry: 0845 606 0265

Pension service: 0800 9912 34, **www.thepensionservice.gov.uk**

Society of trust and estate practitioners: 020 7838 4885

*Your Pension Choice* booklet: 0845 731 3233

# Personal tax data record

National insurance number . . . . . . . . . . . . . . . . . . . . . . . . . . . . . .

State pension number . . . . . . . . . . . . . . . . . . . . . . . . . . . . . . . . .

Tax reference number . . . . . . . . . . . . . . . . . . . . . . . . . . . . . . . . .

Tax office address . . . . . . . . . . . . . . . . . . . . . . . . . . . . . . . . . . .

Tax office telephone number . . . . . . . . . . . . . . . . . . . . . . . . . . . .

2007 tax return sent . . . . . . . . . . . . . . . . . . . . . . . . . . . . . . . . . .

2007 tax return assessment agreed . . . . . . . . . . . . . . . . . . . . . . . . .

2008 tax return sent . . . . . . . . . . . . . . . . . . . . . . . . . . . . . . . . . .

2008 tax return assessment agreed . . . . . . . . . . . . . . . . . . . . . . . . .

Notes on correspondence . . . . . . . . . . . . . . . . . . . . . . . . . . . . . . .

. . . . . . . . . . . . . . . . . . . . . . . . . . . . . . . . . . . . . . . . . . . . . . .

. . . . . . . . . . . . . . . . . . . . . . . . . . . . . . . . . . . . . . . . . . . . . . .

. . . . . . . . . . . . . . . . . . . . . . . . . . . . . . . . . . . . . . . . . . . . . . .

. . . . . . . . . . . . . . . . . . . . . . . . . . . . . . . . . . . . . . . . . . . . . . .

. . . . . . . . . . . . . . . . . . . . . . . . . . . . . . . . . . . . . . . . . . . . . . .

. . . . . . . . . . . . . . . . . . . . . . . . . . . . . . . . . . . . . . . . . . . . . . .

. . . . . . . . . . . . . . . . . . . . . . . . . . . . . . . . . . . . . . . . . . . . . . .

. . . . . . . . . . . . . . . . . . . . . . . . . . . . . . . . . . . . . . . . . . . . . . .

. . . . . . . . . . . . . . . . . . . . . . . . . . . . . . . . . . . . . . . . . . . . . . .

. . . . . . . . . . . . . . . . . . . . . . . . . . . . . . . . . . . . . . . . . . . . . . .

. . . . . . . . . . . . . . . . . . . . . . . . . . . . . . . . . . . . . . . . . . . . . . .

. . . . . . . . . . . . . . . . . . . . . . . . . . . . . . . . . . . . . . . . . . . . . . .

. . . . . . . . . . . . . . . . . . . . . . . . . . . . . . . . . . . . . . . . . . . . . . .

# Contacts and location of documents checklist

Accountant's name and address . . . . . . . . . . . . . . . . . . . . . . . . . . . .

. . . . . . . . . . . . . . . . . . . . . . . . . . . . . . . . . . . . . . . . . . . . . . . . . . . .

Bank name and address . . . . . . . . . . . . . . . . . . . . . . . . . . . . . . . . .

. . . . . . . . . . . . . . . . . . . . . . . . . . . . . . . . . . . . . . . . . . . . . . . . . . . .

Solicitor's name and address . . . . . . . . . . . . . . . . . . . . . . . . . . . . .

. . . . . . . . . . . . . . . . . . . . . . . . . . . . . . . . . . . . . . . . . . . . . . . . . . . .

Birth, marriage and divorce certificate location . . . . . . . . . . . . . . .

. . . . . . . . . . . . . . . . . . . . . . . . . . . . . . . . . . . . . . . . . . . . . . . . . . . .

Car documents, data, contacts and location . . . . . . . . . . . . . . . . . .

. . . . . . . . . . . . . . . . . . . . . . . . . . . . . . . . . . . . . . . . . . . . . . . . . . . .

Insurance policy data, contacts and location . . . . . . . . . . . . . . . . .

. . . . . . . . . . . . . . . . . . . . . . . . . . . . . . . . . . . . . . . . . . . . . . . . . . . .

Pension scheme data, contacts and location . . . . . . . . . . . . . . . . . .

. . . . . . . . . . . . . . . . . . . . . . . . . . . . . . . . . . . . . . . . . . . . . . . . . . . .

Property/mortgage deeds data, contacts and location . . . . . . . . . . .

. . . . . . . . . . . . . . . . . . . . . . . . . . . . . . . . . . . . . . . . . . . . . . . . . . . .

Share and investment certificates location . . . . . . . . . . . . . . . . . . . .

. . . . . . . . . . . . . . . . . . . . . . . . . . . . . . . . . . . . . . . . . . . . . . . . . . . .

Trust deeds location . . . . . . . . . . . . . . . . . . . . . . . . . . . . . . . . . . . . .

. . . . . . . . . . . . . . . . . . . . . . . . . . . . . . . . . . . . . . . . . . . . . . . . . . . .

Wills held by . . . . . . . . . . . . . . . . . . . . . . . . . . . . . . . . . . . . . . . . . .

. . . . . . . . . . . . . . . . . . . . . . . . . . . . . . . . . . . . . . . . . . . . . . . . . . . .

# National insurance rates and limits 2007–2008

| | |
|---|---|
| **Class 1** employed earner<br>**Standard rate**<br>for non contracted out employees<br>(see note) | **Employees**<br>11 per cent on earnings above £100 a week up to and including earnings of £670 a week, then 1 per cent on all earnings above this figure.<br><br>**Employers**<br>12.8 per cent on earnings above £100.00 a week. |
| **Class 1A**<br>On most benefits given to employees. | 12.8 per cent payable only by employers, based on individual's assessable benefit (see page 58) |
| **Class 1B**<br>PAYE settlement agreements | 12.8 per cent payable by employers |
| **Class 2 Self-employed**<br>Small earnings exemption | £2.20 a week<br>£4,635 a year |
| **Class 3**<br>Voluntary contributions rate | £7.80 a week |
| **Class 4 Self-employed**<br><br>Lower limit of profits<br>Upper limit of profits | 8 per cent between £5,225 and £34,840 and 1 per cent thereafter<br>£5,225<br>£34,840 |

*Note*
There are lower percentages for contracted-out employees and reduced rates for certain married women and widows holding a certificate of election (CF383), share fishermen and volunteer development workers.

# Working tax credit, child tax credit and child benefit

There are numerous elements making up these tax credits as indicated in Chapter 9.

Note that you will receive a higher rate of working tax credit if you are aged 50 or more and have just returned to work after qualifying for out-of-work benefits; or you are working person disadvantaged from getting a job because of a disability; or you have a severe disability.

If you are eligible for the working tax credit and you pay a registered or approved child minder to look after your child and you work at least 16 hours a week, you may be able to get a contribution of up to 70 per cent of your costs paid through the working tax credit scheme.

The figures below are per year unless stated otherwise.

| **Working tax credit** | 2007–2008 | 2008–2009 |
| --- | --- | --- |
| | £ | £ |
| Basic element | 1,730 | 1,800 |
| Couple and lone parent element | 1,700 | 1,770 |
| 30 hour element | 705 | 735 |
| Disabled worker element | 2,310 | 2,405 |
| Severe disability element | 980 | 1,020 |
| 50+ Return to work payment (16–29 hours) | 1,185 | 1,235 |
| 50+ Return to work payment (30+ hours) | 1,770 | 1,840 |

**Childcare element of the working tax credit**

| | | |
| --- | --- | --- |
| Maximum eligible cost for one child | £175 per week | £175 per week |
| Maximum eligible cost for two or more children | £300 per week | £300 per week |
| Percentage of eligible costs covered | 80 per cent | 80 per cent |

| **Child tax credit** | 2007–2008 | 2008–2009 |
| --- | --- | --- |
| | £ | £ |
| Family element | 545 | 545 |
| Family element, baby addition | 545 | 545 |
| Child element | 1,845 | 2,085 |
| Disabled child element | 2,440 | 2,540 |
| Severely disabled child element | 980 | 1,020 |

## Income thresholds and withdrawal rates

| | 2007–2008 £ | 2008–2009 £ |
|---|---|---|
| First income threshold | 5,220 | 6,420 |
| First withdrawal rate (per cent) | 37% | 39% |
| Second income threshold | 50,000 | 50,000 |
| Second withdrawal rate (per cent) | 6.67% | 6.67% |
| First threshold for those entitled to child tax credit only | 14,155 | 15,575 |
| Income disregard | 25,000 | 25,000 |

## Child benefit and guardian's allowance rates

| | 2007–2008 £ per week | 2008–2009 £ per week |
|---|---|---|
| Eldest/only child | 18.10 | 18.80 |
| Other children | 12.10 | 12.55 |
| Guardian's allowance | 12.95 | 13.45 |

# Stamp taxes and duties

## Transfers of land and buildings (consideration paid)

| | Residential in disadvantaged areas | Residential outside disadvantaged areas | Non-residential areas |
|---|---|---|---|
| 0% | £0–£150,000 | £0–£125,000 | £0–150,000 |
| 1% | £150,000–£250,000 | £125,000–£250,000 | £150,000–£250,000 |
| 3% | £250,000–£500,000 | £250,000–£500,000 | £250,000–£500,000 |
| 4% | Over £500,000 | Over £500,000 | Over £500,000 |

Residential zero-carbon homes up to £500,000 have a nil stamp duty from 1 October 2007.

# Rates of tax and allowances

| | 2008–2009 | 2007–2008 | 2006–2007 |
|---|---|---|---|
| **Income tax** | | | |
| Starting rate at 10 per cent | – | £2,230 | £2,150 |
| Basic rate at 20 per cent | £0–£36,000 | – | – |
| Basic rate at 22 per cent | – | £2,231–£34,600 | £2,151–£33,300 |
| Higher rate at 40 per cent | over £36,000 | over £34,600 | over £33,300 |

For 2006–2007 and 2007–2008, once the starting rate income band has been used, *savings income* (excluding dividends) is taxed at 20 per cent (not basic rate) if you are a basic rate taxpayer; once your income takes you into the higher-rate band then savings are taxed at 40 per cent.

For 2008–2009 there will be a new 10 per cent starting rate for savings income only, with a limit of £2,320. If an individual's taxable non-savings income is above this limit then the 10 per cent savings rate will not be applicable.

*Dividend income* remains taxed at 10 per cent for basic rate taxpayers and 32.5 per cent for higher rate taxpayers for all the above years.

| **Capital gains tax** | | | |
|---|---|---|---|
| Exemption limit – individuals | £9,600 | £9,200 | £8,800 |
| Exemption limit – trustees | £4,800 | £4,600 | £4,400 |
| Tax rate | 18 per cent | ** | ** |

*Note* **At an individual's top tax rate.

| **Inheritance tax** | | | |
|---|---|---|---|
| Exemption limit | £312,000 | £300,000 | £285,000 |

| **Personal allowance** | £5,435 | £5,225 | £5,035 |
|---|---|---|---|

| **Age allowance** | | | |
|---|---|---|---|
| Aged 65–74 personal | £9,030 | £7,550 | £7,280 |
| married couple's | *†£6,535 | *†£6,285 | *†£6,065 |
| Aged 75 personal | £9,180 | £7,690 | £7,420 |
| and over married couple's | *†£6,625 | *†£6,365 | *†£6,135 |
| Minimum amount | *£2,540 | *£2,440 | *£2,350 |
| Income limit | £21,800 | £20,900 | £20,100 |

| **Blind person's allowance** | £1,800 | £1,730 | £1,660 |
|---|---|---|---|

*Notes* *Relief restricted to 10 per cent, †If born before 6 April 1935.

| **Corporation tax** | | | |
|---|---|---|---|
| Full rate | 28 per cent | 30 per cent | 30 per cent |
| Small companies starting rate for profits up to: | | | |
| £10,000 | 21 per cent | 20 per cent | 19 per cent |
| £50,001–£300,000 | 21 per cent | 20 per cent | 19 per cent |

There is marginal relief for 2007–2008 between £300,000 and £1,500,000 at 1/40. The fraction for 2008–2009 is 7/400.

# Index